5/93

WITHDRAWN

Teaching creative writing

Teaching creative writing

Theory and practice

edited by
Moira Monteith and
Robert Miles

Open University Press
Buckingham • Philadelphia

Open University Press
Celtic Court
22 Ballmoor
Buckingham
MK18 1XW

and
1900 Frost Road, Suite 101
Bristol, PA 19007, USA

First Published 1992

A catalogue record of this book is available
from the British Library

Library of Congress Cataloging-in-Publication Data

Teaching creative writing: theory and practice/edited by Moira
   Monteith and Robert Miles.
       p. cm.
   Includes index.
   ISBN 0–335–15685–1 – ISBN 0–335–15684–3 (pbk.)
   1. English language – Rhetoric – Study and teaching. 2. Creative
writing – Study and teaching. I. Monteith, Moira. II. Miles,
Robert, 1953–
PE1404.T392   1992
808′.042′07 – dc20   91–43046
                                                            CIP

Typeset in 10/11.5pt Baskerville by
Graphicraft Typesetters Ltd., Hong Kong
Printed in Great Britain by St Edmundsbury Press Ltd
Bury St Edmunds, Suffolk

Contents

List of contributors

Peter Abbs is Senior Lecturer at the University of Sussex, where he directs the MA course, Language, the Arts and Education. He is the editor of the Falmer Press Library on Aesthetic Education and author most recently of *Icons of Time: An Experiment in Autobiography,* 1991.

Janet Burroway, McKenzie Professor of English at Florida State University, is the author of seven novels, including *Raw Silk, Opening Nights* and, most recently, *Cutting Stone.* Her textbook, *Writing Fiction,* now in its third edition, is the most widely adopted book of its kind, used in more than 300 colleges and universities in the United States.

David Craig lives in Cumbria and teaches creative writing at Lancaster University. His most recent books are *On the Crofters' Trail,* Cape, a novel, *King Cameron,* Carcanet, and a book of poems, *The Grasshopper's Burden,* is due from Littlewood Arc.

Philip Hobsbaum founded and ran writers' groups in Cambridge, London, Belfast and Glasgow. His most recent publications are *A Reader's Guide to Robert Lowell* and, as editor, *Wordsworth: Selected Poetry and Prose.* He is Titular Professor of English Literature at Glasgow University.

Michael Mangan is a lecturer in English and drama at the University of Sheffield. His writings include books on Shakespeare and Marlowe as well as plays for both stage and radio.

George Marsh is the author of *Teaching Through Poetry: Writing and the Drafting Process,* Hodder and Stoughton, 1988. He has taught on the well-established creative writing course in the English department at the West Sussex Institute of HE and at Portsmouth Polytechnic.

Joan Michelson is Associate Senior Lecturer in English, responsible for the Writing Workshop at Wolverhampton Polytechnic. She has published essays, stories, poems and two non-fiction books, including *From Bergen–Belsen to Baghdad*, Mosaic Press, Canada 1992.

Robert Miles teaches creative writing and literature in the English Studies section of Sheffield City Polytechnic. He is the author of *Gothic Writing 1750–1825: A Genealogy*, Routledge, 1992.

Moira Monteith was one of the team of lecturers who first introduced creative writing units in the English Studies degree at Sheffield City Polytechnic. Recent publications include *Ringing the Changes* (with G. Dyer and G. Mitchell) Routledge, 1991 and *Computers and Language* (ed.) Intellect Books, 1992.

Jane Rogers is the author of four novels, including *Her Living Image* and *Mr. Wroe's Virgins*, Faber, and an award-winning TV drama. She has held writing residencies at Northern College, Sheffield City Polytechnic and Cambridge University, and taught creative writing at Liverpool University and Manchester Polytechnic.

Nick Rogers teaches 'A' level English. He has organized writing workshops over many years.

John Singleton teaches creative writing at Crewe and Alsager College of Higher Education. He has published fiction for both adults and children.

Introduction

Robert Miles and Moira Monteith

The simplest way of introducing this volume of essays on the theory and practice of teaching creative writing is to describe how it came into being.

As teachers on a polytechnic degree course with a significant, assessed, creative writing component, we felt the strong need of a student 'text'. We felt it would be helpful for our practice to have a book, half anthology, half commentary, in which examples of canonical and contemporary writing were mixed with critical discussion. So that, if one were working, say, in a creative writing seminar on metre, one would have a preliminary discussion on the nature and importance of rhythm in poetry, supplemented by a variety of examples. The need was partly 'natural' (ready material being part of the natural economy of teaching) and partly 'artificial', as tutors constantly came up against the problem of copyright in supplying examples of modern practice. On our course we still feel the need of such a text, even if some of the problems have been alleviated by institutional and individual agreements on copyright.

The principal reason such a text did not come into being was that, although publishers' readers constantly approved the idea, there was also continual doubt about whether a market for such a text actually existed. We were thus faced with the paradox of publishers and readers agreeing that, owing to curricular and institutional changes, creative writing was a growth area, but that, in terms of student numbers, the market was not yet ready. We resolved this paradox by switching our market to an area of indisputable demand: to those higher education (HE) and further education (FE) lecturers in established writing courses as well as teachers of Alternative 'A' level courses, and to those in the process of planning new courses which might include a writing component. Our experience of the Verbal Arts Association and Northern Association of Writers in Education had convinced us that such a market existed.

As a consequence we sent a preamble outlining a somewhat different project to teachers and writers we thought might have an interest. The burden of this preamble was an invitation to consider how, in the current, curricular flux, they might best assist their colleagues, either by contributing to the 'theory' of creative writing, and thus shoring up its academic credentials in a still sceptical environment, or by giving concrete examples of what they did. In this way the subject could be strengthened through the sharing of good practice. We have been delighted by the response we received. The range of experience of our contributors, which covers the spectrum of creative writing in further and higher education, is particularly noteworthy.

At this point we must acknowledge a debt of gratitude to the readers appointed by the Open University Press. They helpfully put their collective fingers on a number of crucial themes which have found development in this book, partly as a result of their intervention, and partly because they are part of the furniture of what we feel this book identifies as an area of emerging debate. The readers urged us to cover the wide scope of practice in teaching creative writing and to give special attention to the problems of assessment. They also identified a latent tension inherent in the proposal, that between the 'academic' teaching of writing and writing as an activity or subject (the debate problematizes these terms) 'taught' in its own right. Simply, it is the difference between creative writing as a component in an English Literature degree and, more radically, creative writing as a distinct and independent discipline. As George Marsh, Nick Rogers, Janet Burroway and Peter Abbs note, creative writing is not a subject, a body of knowledge to be transmitted but an activity in which the 'personal' and the 'imagination' are indivisible.

It is, of course, a very old debate, witness its avatars: classic/romantic; nurture/nature; art/genius. To employ Seamus Heaney's words (coincidentally invoked by both Nick Rogers and Philip Hobsbaum), it is the difference between 'craft' and 'technique', cleverness with words and the use of words informed by 'the whole creative effort of the mind's and body's resources . . .'. At the risk of being flippantly short, it is the difference between 'creative' with a large or small 'c'. As contributors' attitudes vary on this issue, so varies their conception of the role of creative writing, how it is best 'taught', how matters are best arranged for it to happen, and how it is best accommodated within the institution.

We think it true (and fair) to say, as the editors, that this debate initially fluttered on the edge of our peripheral vision (although perhaps less distantly so in the case of Moira Monteith). Caught up with the historically embattled position of creative writing, we had our eyes fixed on arguments defending its legitimacy, thus forgetting, or missing, the fact that the argument had moved on, that creative writing, having found its feet, was capable of making more positive sounds, not simply justifying itself in relation to the historically accidental shape of 'English', but setting out its own agenda, creating its own debate about what it is, and how it ought best to move forward.

We believe the emergence of a debate, of difference among the contributors, is a resounding good. Where we initially imagined the debate falling between 'traditionalists' and 'innovators' quarrelling over the admission of creative writing, we have, gratifyingly, a more diverse scene. For instance, Robert Miles's curricular defence of creative writing as having, academically, at the very least, credentials equal with those of 'prac. crit.', credentials owing to creative writing's critically beneficial focus on 'craft' (a view also proposed by Philip Hobsbaum), is in stark collision with arguments made by George Marsh. Many of the differences may be accounted for by the varying experiences of the contributors: those teaching creative writing to aspiring critics on a BA in 'English' will have different attitudes from those, say, teaching 'A' level students, many of whom will take the subject no further than that, and these attitudes will be different again from those belonging to colleagues teaching aspiring teachers. This variety suggests that the teaching of creative writing is developing on several, mutually communicating fronts.

Despite the invitation to contributors to think about creative writing in terms of theory and/or practice, we have not formally divided the essays in this book in that way, largely because the essays constantly move back and forth between the two. However, there is an order to the essays, a movement from the general to the particular.

Moira Monteith's chapter considers the use of the term 'creative writing' and discusses its problematic nature and the social pressures which led some educationists to avoid its use. She looks at the place of creative writing within higher education, schools and the community at large. Three series of reports dealing with English teaching are included in the survey: Board of Education Circulars (1910 and 1912), *A Language for Life*, published by the Bullock Committee (1975) and the Cox Report presented to the Secretary of State for Education and Science (1989), immediately following the Kingman Report and preceding the publication of the National Curriculum. Government intervention and its relationship to the desired changes in literacy levels as the necessity to raise workforce skills increases is compared with the remarkably stable courses in universities. However it now seems probable that HE courses in English will change to accommodate students fresh from the Alternative 'A' level syllabuses growing in popularity and follow the line of some new courses taught in polytechnics and colleges of HE. Revolutionary changes in new technology are under way and these will have an undoubted effect on the way we write, in both structure and presentation. Moira Monteith presents a scenario for change but believes that 'creative writing' should remain as an entity within new courses.

Philip Hobsbaum begins his chapter: 'Those who study a subject should also study its history.' He traces the different origins of English courses in HE. In Scotland 'the study of English evolved from rhetoric, which was itself a branch of logic and which was therefore taught by philosophers'; whereas English Literature in Victorian England began as an off-shoot of classics and 'was thought to be second-best, studied by women and foreigners and, as such, has never been deeply respected'. Almost from the beginning the majority of students were women, and yet the courses have been 'designed by male academics for male students'. The encouragement of composition is going forward, but in a curiously limited way, confined to the form of the critical essay. Philip Hobsbaum believes this is a respectable form but we do not remember writers for that genre but for other writing they may have produced. He argues that there are few critics about whose distinction modern academics would agree and concludes that criticism is a hard practice to follow. He draws a comparison with students of music, architecture and painting who, unlike students of literature are encouraged to practise their craft. He maintains English Literature courses are trapped in a time-warp; they have included the study of philology but not the writing that was part of the old classics teaching. He goes on to propose appointing writers permanently to the staff in university departments and wishes to balance the teaching of criticism with the craft of writing. He concludes with a fascinating example of a 'working' discussion where several writers offer opinions on another's work.

Robert Miles's chapter assesses the potential, future role of a creative writing component in an English curriculum under pressure from developments in contemporary theory and from institutional changes. In particular he argues that there is a positive tension between the drift of contemporary theory and the pull of creative writing, a tendency for the two to work first with, then against each other, a state of affairs he sums up in the phrase 'tensed complementariness', and which he sees as the basis of good curricular practice within the arts. He considers the current situation as regards critical studies where he believes 'culture' has replaced the text as the primary object of study. On the other hand, creative writing replaces the author 'as the mind at the centre of the text'. It affords the student the opportunity of comparing theories of how texts come into being with the actual experience of bringing texts into being. He also discusses practical issues concerning workshops, in particular student involvement in criticizing each other's work. He raises the question that writing workshops concentrating on poetry may well be different in their relationship to theory from those which concentrate on prose.

George Marsh examines the variety of aims and methods of assessment in the teaching of literary writing. He believes that 'sympathetic response is at the heart of the teaching and learning' and that this may be lost if students just receive a mark. He considers seven aims in all:

1 'To train professional writers'. Criterion-referencing would be an appropriate form of assessment, to be preferred to the present degree classi-
fications. Assessment should include feedback at several stages of the
drafting process and sampling from a portfolio of work.

2 'To illuminate criticism by learning experientially about the construction
of a text'. Courses with such aims would be unsuccessful in practice,
tutors awarding high grades for mechanically correct work.

3 'To develop communication skills'. He considers these extremely valuable for the students who can still engage in literary writing since this is
'more motivating . . . at the most demanding level'. Assessment should
be concerned in this case with efficiency and the skill level revealed.

4 'That learners do literary writing because it is intrinsically worthwhile'.
He claims this is 'the real aim of those of us who are teaching it because
we love it'. However final grading may get in the way of true encouragement and staff may fall into the trap of believing they can 'assign a
numerical value to the quality of mind of every professional recruit in
the country'.

5 'To teach literary writing'. This would be unsuccessful in a Creative Arts
Programme.

6 'To develop the mind of the student' or 'to develop imagination and
creativity'. This allows a great deal of leeway – and the skills can be
considered transferable and assessment can be whatever is deemed
appropriate.

7 'To prepare school-teachers for teaching creative writing'. He considers
this an adequate and useful aim for a professional end. Throughout the
chapter he argues strongly for some version of criterion-referencing to be
introduced.

Janet Burroway writes about the American experience of creative writing
courses, both nationally and from a personal viewpoint. She begins with
a first-person account of learning prosody on winter afternoons with her
literature teacher at school. She then discusses the development of these
courses which began 'as early as the turn of the century'. She traces their
progress towards legitimacy within university departments and cites her
own institution where over half the students now in the English department
are writing students. She gives a teacher's eye view of her writing class, all
with a desire to write but with varying ability. Some will succeed but she
feels it is impossible to predict at this stage which students will do so.
Originally committed to the 'star system' she waited for the 'star student'
who 'would provide the raison d'être of my teaching'. She now feels a sense
of ambivalence: are teachers producing a host of untalented writers or are
they 'the monks of the new dark ages, keeping the language alive in our
workshop cloisters'? Despite the current backlash against creative writing
courses in the United States she believes creative writing (as well as literature)

needs to be taught since neither is part 'of the everyday experience of most people'. Students seem to have learnt certain techniques from their wealth of television watching and are keen to use language in writing, perhaps because they have such little practice in personal writing, now that letters are a dead form. Creative writing is one of the surrogates for war, just as sport is, and should be encouraged for that reason alone. She modestly hopes her students will end up with 'a better sense of the relationship between their language and their truth than the President of the United States'.

John Singleton discusses the beginning and development of the very well organized course in writing at Crewe and Alsager College of Higher Education. He looks at writing and assessment as a concern of 'curriculum politics' and gives a very interesting account of the way the course came into being, its flexibility in terms of other courses and validating bodies so that its 'evolution . . . has been as much casual and opportunistic as deliberate cultivation'. The lecturers gave no hostages to fortune by using the word 'creative' in the title of the course. He quotes specifically from the course document so that anyone in comparable institutions thinking of establishing a similar course would find this invaluable. Not satisfied with the establishment and maintenance of an innovatory course the staff have gone on to develop their methods of assessment. They have moved to a position whereby assessment can be negotiated and believe this will encourage independent and active learning. The assessment is evolving in a way more beneficial to the learner than the teacher – a salutary reflection on George Marsh's strictures about academics and the status they feel comes from awarding marks. At Crewe and Alsager, 'assessment is far more differential, sensitive to the nature of the subject, the experience of the students, and matched to the subject's defined learning outcomes'.

Peter Abbs takes up one of the aims discussed by George Marsh, and looks at the place of creative writing in the development of teachers. English students on the Postgraduate Certificate in Education (PGCE) course at the University of Sussex undertake a writing unit as part of their training. Like other contributors, Peter Abbs talks of the changing nature of workshop sessions and the 'volatile perceptions' of a workshop's members. His aims for the course were to allow students 'ample experience of writing', knowledge of the process of composition and direct experience of performance. 'It was time for the students to have first-hand experience of the poetic rather than the discursive'. He suggests that too much theory encourages 'dissociation between the intellectual and the personal'. He includes a wealth of examples from the students' own writing during the course and incorporates student comment from their journal on the work undertaken. He ends what is, in his own words, 'a very pragmatic account', with a brief statement about the philosophy underlying this course. People should be able to 'develop lives of inner significance and communal value'; he goes on to exemplify this in political, educational and spiritual terms. It is interesting to compare this view with that in the Cox Report, which does indeed give writing a central place in educational and even political terms. It does, however, neglect the spiritual, perhaps another concept connected with creativity and about which many people feel slightly uncomfortable.

Nick Rogers covers the changing face of 'A' level, with its new opportunities and changing demands for creative writing. Several 'A' level examination boards currently allow submission of creative writing work which may account for as much as a quarter of the final marks. He comments on the differences noted when students are writing within the context of courses predominantly given over either to literary study or to language. He also discusses a question not really addressed elsewhere in this book: that of perceived development from one stage to another, in this case from General Certificate of Secondary Education (GCSE) to 'A' level. He suggests ways of approaching workshops, particularly when students are sometimes inexperienced both at writing and at criticizing each other's work. He considers the inclusion of a commentary on students' own original writing. He believes there will be continuing pressure on the privileged status of literary forms and that other forms of discourse will have to be included in creative writing courses.

Jane Rogers represents the crucial contribution made by professional writers who bring their valuable experience to teaching. Her chapter looks at teaching from a professional writer's point of view. She believes students should consider 'the specific problems and tasks that a writer faces in constructing a story, poem, whatever' and that a useful method for solving these problems is 'raiding and copying from other writers'. She refreshingly comments on her increasing jaundice with 'inspiration' and 'self-expression' and 'creativity' since the thought of them can 'induce imaginative paralysis'. She does not believe you can teach inspiration; 'you can set up situations where you hope to inspire students'; and 'what can be taught are techniques; the tricks and skills a writer uses'. Accordingly she looks at the craft of being a writer, concentrating on novels and short stories. She considers beginnings, plots, characterization, setting and dialogue by considering particular literary examples. She also discusses style, including parody. She ends by saying that these examples should not be seen as a list of rules and prescriptions; 'there are no rules'. Instead she advises the student 'to try on styles and techniques like hats, and see what they do for you'.

Joan Michelson also looks at the workshop experience but from a different angle. She gives two vividly described examples of workshop sessions, one a three-hour block from a module taken by second- and third-year Humanities degree students at Wolverhampton Polytechnic, the second a day school offered to adults at a Centre for Continuing Education. In the first session the students discuss a short story by Jorge Luis Borges, they consider the author's 'afterword' and talk about the plot and how it is organized. After a very tight discussion they engage in a 'whimsy' variation of the story before going back to considering Borges's opening paragraph. It is clear the students gain many insights from this discussion and move on to consider the relevance of an author's own comments and the connections of this story with a 'told' story. The second session is different in that the students do not have a text in front of them but have to listen. The story is an adaptation of a folk story, with complex detail but a simple, repetitive structure and some exceedingly effective images. The individuals in the group have to retell the story, perhaps from a different viewpoint. They can use notes for reference but must narrate the story. The story-telling freed at least one student 'from the barricade of the thesaurus, dictionary and polished prose'. Joan Michelson believes that workshops help 'trick our imagination into play'.

Michael Mangan compares ways in which drama techniques relate to the context of the creative writing class. He first looks at workshop games and exercises and particularly considers one which takes account of both creative freedom and artistic restrictions. The improvised, 'word-at-a-time' exercise has a group dynamic aspect as opposed to the lonely, often antisocial activity of writing. The game opens up areas of imaginative territory, an exploration of a group 'subconscious'. This can be very helpful for individual students since they do not, indeed cannot, try to be impressive, sometimes a problem in writing courses. They have to learn, however, that they alone cannot control the narrative but instead have to concentrate on a flexible response to others' contributions. They subsequently learn that to improve the game and to arrive at an interesting narrative they must devise some rules. So they gain the perception that rules can be creative and not only restrictive. The students are also concerned with the predictability of the narrative and the way it unfolds through time. Michael Mangan also gives an example of material for a workshop, in this case a poorly constructed scene from a 'play'. The purpose of the subsequent discussion would be to help students avoid mistakes and become aware of the need for craftsmanship through a consideration of its absence. This is a kind of reverse exercise to those in Jane Rogers's chapter, where she looks at effective uses of the author's craft. Michael Mangan's aim, however, is essentially the same: 'to offer a way of discovering for themselves the kinds of rules, principles and techniques which will work best for them'.

David Craig looks at the workshop approach, discussing a month's work with his MA group. He first gives an account of a writing weekend the group spent together. He includes comments on students' reading and then a joint exercise by the group, using guidelines he has devised (and borrowed). He evokes most effectively the creative situation of such weekends where people write, and think about writing, even while they are cooking or sharing a pot of tea. He wonders if the friendliness obvious at such weekends makes criticism more difficult, but then there are other workshops for that. He comments on books published by ex-students, 'the best evidence of what can be done'. He comments that when they write '*to* each other' they write more comedy, and that much comedy writing is in fact collaborative. He includes critiques of students' writing as well as details of a group publication which will involve the students in writing accounts of their experiences on the Lancaster writing course. Throughout the chapter he brings alive the pleasure of writing as well as the difficulties and indicates the nature of some workshops, the enjoyment that comes from sharing the problems of publication.

We trust we have said enough for readers to have a fair idea of the themes and topics they will encounter in this book. We hope it conveys some of the spirit and vigour evident to anyone who examines the situation of creative writing today. Courses continue to proliferate and there is now a potential continuum in writing experience from early childhood, throughout secondary school, continuing and higher education as well as further degrees. The need for informed debate about teaching and learning methodology in this area is vital. We trust this book goes some way towards encouraging fruitful discussion as well as sharing some of the ideas and experiences we have found helpful.

We believe that the 'crisis in English Studies' encouraged the breaking down of barriers. A crisis, of course, is a crossroads and only those nostalgically hearkening after where they have been need think of crisis as a moment of pending doom. Some crises are indeed calamitous, others creative. We think we speak for many when we say that the 'crisis in English Studies' has provoked a period of change and rejuvenation, of renewal and vigour. So it is generally with debate, with difference. Rather than itemize differences among the contributors, we invite the readers to experience for themselves the ferment of a common purpose in debate with itself.

1

Creative writing:
A historical perspective

Moira Monteith

creative
1.a. Having the quality of creating, given to creating; of or pertaining to creation; originative.
b. Spec. of literature and art, thus also of a writer or artist: inventive, imaginative; exhibiting imagination as well as intellect, and thus differentiated from the merely critical, 'academic', journalistic, professional, mechanical, etc. in literary or artistic production. So **creative writing,** such writing: also freq. in the U.S. as a course of study.

Why bother with the term 'creative writing' at all?

'Creative writing' exists as a name among the lexicon of terms known by teachers and lecturers from the arts and humanities section of the educational spectrum. Nomenclature concerning writing, useful for teaching purposes, is not abundant, particularly if we include only that which is widely acceptable. Specific terminology is necessary if we wish to know and agree what we are talking about, as virtually every report on teaching English or language has stated. It is true that successive reports have increased the variety of terms but some of these have fallen subsequently into disuse. 'Creative writing' has had a short but interesting history. Its usage is clearly problematic. In this chapter I want to tease out some of the problems associated with the term and its use at all levels of education. Such an analysis reveals the problems our society faces with the notion of creativity in general and very specifically its function within the educational curriculum.

Language features significantly in our own concept of identity, national and regional, as well as regards our views of community, gender and race;

and since language is at the very crux of our being, discussion concerning it stirs up emotional reactions. Such responses are also evident when it comes to considering English as a curriculum subject. Writing is frozen language in the sense that it does not run away and disappear into the ground as speech tends to do, but can be considered at more length and evaluated more easily. This explains why writing is and has been seen as such a useful strategy for assessment. It is not too emphatic to say writing is at the heart of the debate about social control in education and social engineering, of concern about the artistic and the vocational, of the creative and the judgemental. This last concern is fully developed in Philip Hobsbaum's chapter. Writing is one of the few learning and teaching areas that run through every level of society, from pre-school learning to continuing education classes and community outreach courses, a lifelong continuum of practice and study. Writing embraces both the old and the new, the study of very old texts and the latest developments in new technology which allow a writer access to more information than writers of previous generations ever had, to capacities for designing, recrafting and altering texts not possible before. 'Creative writing' is a subset of writing in general. We shy away from the phrase at the moment, mainly because it has been tied to political implications about ways of teaching but also because it may seem ineffectual, since writing in journals such as the *New Scientist* could be considered creative work just as much as a short story. I think it is important to look at this current taboo and examine the attitudes behind it. I suggest we need to retain the term.

The definition from the *Oxford English Dictionary* (*OED*) above finds examples of the use of 'creative writing' as far back as 1922 and refers to an article in the *English Journal* (an American publication) in 1930 on courses in creative writing. Such references no doubt led to the dictionary determination that such courses must be American. The use of 'merely' in the definition signals the contentious question of value judgements: who differentiates between the imaginative and the 'merely critical' and is it possible to do this effectively? A subsequent coinage, quoted in 1973, of '**creative accounting**' – 'applied to financial or other strategies which are imaginative or ingenious, esp. in a misleading fashion' – indicates the difficulty we have in approving creativity. The definition fits rather well with the notion that original thinking is suspect and often used for 'wrong' ends. No wonder that institutions such as Crewe and Alsager College (see Chapter 6) and Sheffield City Polytechnic decided not to use the word 'creative' when designing writing courses which had to be validated by the Council for National Academic Awards (CNAA).

A dichotomy of creativity versus discipline runs deep beneath the educational values promoted at any one time. Sometimes theorists acknowledge the division openly, even calling on classical antecedents such as Dionysus and Apollo, but often the tension is revealed in the kind of contemporary policies promoted or pragmatic practices followed. For example, the survey of schools undertaken as part of the Bullock Report, *A Language for Life* (1975) revealed that in secondary schools the pupils who were considered less able had to undertake more 'exercises' to improve their command of English and were taught less literature. Although no overt theory could be held responsible for such an educational division, practice revealed a general acceptance sufficiently broad to give it the status of an inbuilt social ideology.

I do not intend to spend time and space defining 'creative writing' myself. The term continues to exist because people use it (for example, the current education database ERIC includes 943 references) and, as Terry Eagleton states when he is trying to define 'literary' and 'literature', 'these terms will not really do but . . . we have no better ones at the moment'.[1] There is probably a general consensus on what creative writing is and what a creative writing course might entail but problems arise with the associations, sometimes apparently irrelevant and sometimes pejorative, with which it is burdened. I suggest that creative writing is at the nexus of a number of tensions within our educational system. Our attitude towards it reveals our prejudices just as our attitude towards dialects reveals more than a like or dislike for a particular way of speaking. It is important to keep the term in mind, whatever adjectives we may or may not use, when we need to design new courses and to defend the position of established ones.

Creative writing in higher education

English, contained within the arts/humanities section of the curriculum, is able to attract a large number of students but so far has set its face against directly vocational courses and prefers to encourage 'transferable skills' as a way of meeting the career aims of the students and the needs of employers. English itself is currently in turmoil as a HE discipline, its defenders unsure whether to embrace gladly the current position of widely differing courses and approaches and accommodate the problems of 'impurity' and lack of cohesion this entails or to state that the real way forward is via one approach, for example critical theory.

As a subject in university courses English has been left remarkably un-trammelled and has tended to remain very stable. The canon of texts has altered slightly following salvos from feminist and other critics and as a result of new ways of analysing texts. On the whole, though, the courses have remained relatively unchanged and the basic structure and study recognizable for decades. This climate has not left much room for innovation. In HE creative writing often consists of a few 'optional' units taught within a degree structure which focuses on literary criticism. It is interesting to note perhaps that the one part of our binary system which has had less 'interference' than the rest has opted for stability. Real change has originated and developed in the 5–16 years' section of our education system as regards

English, where the desire for government regulation is strongest and the debate is fiercest.

Polytechnics and colleges of higher education had to have their courses validated, often by the CNAA. These validation exercises, often lengthy, time consuming and sometimes absurd, nevertheless encouraged the growth of different amalgamations of course units. John Singleton describes the building up of such a course at Crewe and Alsager. However, writing courses in themselves are not monolithic. They shade into the somewhat unknown (in HE) area of courses in journalism and publishing. Many jobs, both now and in the near future, will place a high priority on writing skills and a vocational bent may be one way out of the current cul-de-sac for English. The new 'publishing set' which is a major part of a degree course at Middlesex Polytechnic is one example of this shift. Writing tutors may then find themselves defending the practice of writing poems and short stories within the structure of Communication Studies or Publishing degrees. They may need to make some accommodation to the growth of video as an art form and the development of multi-media as one strategy for creating artistic works. Creative writing is a 'growth point' not just in the fact that it can attract students but in the original meaning of the phrase, the place where the cells are actively dividing. Many new shoots of growth can develop from or within it. It is therefore impossible to view creative writing as a stable subject. Writing courses will expand in HE, in one way or another. The debate about what topics should be included and the position of 'creative writing' within these courses will prove exceedingly interesting.

English as a school subject

English in schools has been and is viewed in a different light to English as a university discipline and even as an 'A' level course which was developed and maintained as an entrance qualification for university work. It has always been seen as an important subject in school and is now one of the bases of the National Curriculum. It is a straddling subject, vocational in some modes and indeed employers' needs as regards literacy are frequently invoked. Literature, usually an integral part of English but sometimes seen as an important but separate element, is not vocationally oriented. Writing as an activity also straddles the boundaries, dealing with items such as business letters and reports as well as the production of poems, short stories, plays and autobiographical pieces. The correct balance at any one time between the vocational and non-vocational elements (though the division is often not quite so crudely drawn) has called forth many reports from government departments and other educational bodies, who clearly felt the need to advise on this area. I intend to look at what the Bullock and Cox reports have to say about writing, with a brief comment on earlier reports of 1910 and 1912, already considered by Jacqueline Rose.[2]

Writing has long been carefully graded in state schools according to its apparent suitability for pupils in view of their differing levels of future employment, from the language considered appropriate in 'object lessons' to the titles of compositions pupils were required to write. In 1915 and earlier, class distinctions as perceived by educationists led to different expectations as regards language use. A Board of Education circular of 1912 was concerned with education for elementary school children, that is most children up to the age of 14, excluding secondary and private schools. It advised the teacher 'to preserve and develop naturally the unsophisticated virtues of children's language . . . He need not revert to "childish" language, but if he can recover some of the directness and simplicity of thought and expression which education too often impairs, he will find that his effort has been of as great advantage to himself as to the children' (BOE 1912: 31-2).[3] Yet a previous report dealing with English in secondary schools (for selected children, usually paid for by parents) stated: 'The instruction in English in a Secondary School aims at training the mind to appreciate English literature, and at cultivating the power of using the English language in speech and writing . . . Without training in the use of language, literature cannot be fully understood or properly appreciated. Without the study of literature there can be no mastery over language' (BOE 1910: 3). Matthew Arnold had already noted in 1899 in a comparison of children's letters the distinction in styles of writing resulting from such teaching. The 1912 circular also stated: 'No attempt should be make to impose a difference in style in written and oral composition' for the ordinary school pupil.

These Board of Education circulars intended children to be taught language and writing according to the kind of school they attended. It seems almost as if one group, the majority of all pupils in fact, should remain 'unimpaired' by education, their simplicity of thought and expression suitable for their station in life. Children then needed just enough literacy to work well in the factories, mills and shops but as far as possible should be unchanged by their learning. Clearly such an educational premise was unworkable if not untenable as society changed. 'Power' and 'mastery over language' reserved for the minority of pupils in 1910 became essential for the majority in an articulate workforce, particularly after the Second World War when the 1944 Education Act brought in secondary education for all.

Periodically government ministers, the media and, to a varying degree, the general public become apprehensive about the standards of education, and in particular that of literacy, attained by pupils in the state education system. There seems no evidence that standards do fall. Indeed the number of examination passes attained at 'O' level and GCSE indicate creditable improvement. It is more likely therefore that the literacy requirements expected within an industrial nation rise as skill levels required of the workforce rise. The periodic bouts of anxiety over standards reveal another hitching up of reading and writing levels deemed necessary for the average pupil on leaving school to enter employment.

If we examine the publicity surrounding the establishment of the Bullock Committee of Inquiry and subsequently the Kingman and Cox reports, we notice that particular arguments recur. One line of reasoning is concerned with what grammar is and the way it should be taught. Another line of argument links allegedly suspect pedagogical theories with a variety of teaching approaches in order to condemn them. 'Reading with real books' is currently under attack, just as the indiscipline associated with creative writing was condemned in the 1970s. One reference will indicate this continuing climate of opinion. John Rae, Headmaster of Westminster School (1970–86) and a recent columnist in the *Times Educational Supplement* stated: 'The overthrow of grammar coincided with the acceptance of the equivalent of creative writing in social behaviour. As nice points of grammar were mockingly dismissed as pedantic and irrelevant, so was punctiliousness in such matters as honesty, responsibility, property, gratitude, apology and so on.'[4]

The Committee of Inquiry chaired by Sir Alan Bullock was established originally in 1972 by the then Minister of Education, Margaret Thatcher, to see if there were any evidence for a claim that reading standards were falling. Its brief was widened subsequently to 'language in education' (Introduction, xxxi). The report had a defensive stance therefore on certain issues, and it is hardly surprising that the Bullock Committee wanted no taint of the 'permissive'.

It is interesting to see how the creative is contextualized in the report: 'We received many letters which suggested that "creativity" is now reverenced and that "formal" work has virtually been banished' (1.8). The strong opposition between 'reverenced' and 'banished' is reflected in the following statement: 'It is commonly believed that English in most primary schools today consists largely of creative writing, free reading, topic or project work, and improvised drama, and that spelling and formal language work have no place.' 'Creative', 'free' and 'improvised' are counterpointed by 'formal', though it is by no means clear who holds the common belief. The committee decided to find out if the common belief were true. 'How general has been the shift of emphasis away from the formal to the "permissive"? . . . The answers we received certainly did not reveal a picture of the decay of such work [formal practice] in the midst of a climate of unchecked creativity.' The division seems clear. There is no suggestion of a balanced or disciplined structure to creative work. Instead such work is associated with immediate inspiration from a particular stimulus (the old 'object lesson' turned on its head) and improvization. It appears to be 'free' and 'unchecked'.

Having established this context for creativity the committee looked around for another descriptor for the activity of 'creative' writing. 'Free', 'expression', 'personal' and 'spontaneity' were associated with forms of writing that needed more backbone to survive 'the transition from artlessness to art' (11.5).

While recognizing the problem of a 'lack of agreed definition' the report supported the adoption of three categories of writing based on function: Expressive, Transactional, and Poetic, superimposed upon two modes of use, language in the role of participant and of spectator. The reason for this adoption seems overwhelmingly pedagogic, to overcome 'the difficulty of structuring development in writing'. Problems of linguistic definition surfaced almost immediately but the categories continued in use in advisory documents and in-service training for a considerable time. These categories got rid of the notion of different 'languages' for pupils in different schools or even within streams of one school and encouraged the inclusion of all three categories of writing within every syllabus. The Expressive is 'central . . . "close to the speaker"', relating in fact to the 'unsophisticated virtues of children's language' of the 1912 BOE Report. The Transactional 'demands greater explicitness in the writing, a more pressing concern for accuracy of reference', and clearly is related to other subjects in the curriculum, involving for example writing up science experiments and business letters. The Poetic is granted less definition than the other two categories but longer explanation. This comes in the form of examples, commenting on a child's writing, just as anyone trying to define creative writing might do. The report also commented on 'the importance of the pupil's intention as a writer' and the need for the teacher 'to learn all he can about the processes involved in writing'. These last two items were emphasized in subsequent developments such as the National Writing Project. Although what the committee says about writing in the Poetic mode is very sensible and few teachers would argue with their comments, the name 'Poetic' was never satisfactory nor widely used. One clear difficulty was the lack of enjoyment pupils seemed to find in the poetry lessons endured at school, according to the survey. It was difficult therefore to use this term for challenging, innovative, structured writing. It was just not acceptable as an alternative to 'creative writing'.

Between the Bullock Report and the Cox Report (1989) the teaching of writing developed in a number of ways. There was much greater emphasis on the purpose of writing; children should have their own sense of intention and not write only for the teacher. A sense of audience became more important, so pupils would know that writing was destined to be read, for example, by other pupils, parents, people out in the community, such as in a residential home and not only by the teacher or, occasionally, in the school magazine. Teachers began to consider the process of writing, interweaving stages of composition; conceptualization, the actual writing and subsequent editing were stressed.

Changes also occurred in the examination system. The two-tier approach, 'O' level and the Certificate of Secondary Education (CSE), was already creaking at the time of the Bullock Report. The 'new' CSE boards which had been 'encouraged to experiment much more widely' (11.35) were congratulated for their innovations. Their versions of a language examination provided opportunities for the submission of both course work and 'personal writing' for assessment. This experimentation was later consolidated in the portfolio of work submitted for the GCSE examinations, introduced in 1988.

The late 1980s saw a flurry of reports: Kingman, Cox and the subsequent version printed as part of the National Curriculum (1990), all seeking to regularize how English is to be taught and learnt during the statutory years of education. *English for ages 5 to 16: Proposals of the Secretary of State for Education and Science,* was written by the National Curriculum English Working Group, chaired by Professor Cox. The Cox Report, as it came to be known, was wide-ranging, tolerant of accepted research in teaching and language, and conscious of new social and technological developments. Like all previous reports, it attempted further definition and categorization. This time, for example, it introduced the distinction between chronological and non-chronological writing (17.41) but still retained the use of literary and non-literary writing. It rationalized much further than Bullock the significance of function to writing and, since it consciously preceded the National Curriculum, was task-oriented.

English as a school subject has always included a number of curriculum approaches. The Cox Report clearly exemplified five models (2.20) 'though we stress that they are not the only possible views': personal growth, cross-curricular, adult needs, cultural heritage and cultural analysis. Taking this multi-model basis and drawing on the skills approach to English (listening, speaking, reading, writing) opportunities for writing as part of a pupil's cognitive development should flourish. Writing can be viewed as one stage in scripting, reasoning and reporting without necessarily being seen as the final product. Cox diminished the importance of the written essay, whose dominance, it was alleged, came from its pre-eminence 'as a vehicle for the transmission of knowledge in written examinations' (17.17). Redrafting material was emphasized as well as knowledge of the writer's potential audience. Members of the Working Group selected the section on writing to deal with 'communicating with the outside world and having a say in that world' (17.20). Cox went on to quote from a paragraph in the Kingman Report concerning democracy: 'People need expertise in language to be able to participate effectively in a democracy . . .' The belief in *A Language for Life,* the title of the Bullock Report, was thus extended to include the demands of citizenship: 'people need the resources of language both to defend their rights and to fulfil their obligations' (17.20). Writing is seen not only as a wide-ranging skill with multi-faceted products but as central to an individual's political development.

The Cox Report is a positive document which features writing in a central position, moving it further on from its function as a means of recording and assessing. However students are now faced with a multitude of tasks. Unless teachers recognize some categorization of an area of writing such as 'creative', this kind of writing may feature less frequently within a syllabus. The possibility that less time may be given to creative writing becomes more likely when viewed within the framework of the National Curriculum. For example, there are 14 items in section 31: 'General provisions for key stage 4'. Some are lists: 'write in a wider range of forms, including a number of the following: notes, diaries, personal letters, formal letters, reports, pamphlets, reviews, essays, advertisements, newspaper articles, biography, autobiography, poems, stories, playscripts'. Others indicate a wider, less prescriptive approach: 'have continuing opportunities to write in aesthetic and imaginative ways'. Hard-pressed teachers seeking to include as many items as possible from the National Curriculum document may feel that aesthetic and imaginative ways are sufficiently covered by going through the list.

The National Curriculum does maintain Cox's positive approach towards writing. For example, in the general provision to key stage 1: 'Pupils should see adults writing. Teachers should write alongside pupils, sharing and talking about their writing...' But its present nature is prescriptive, itemizing tasks and this makes it more difficult for teachers and pupils to take a developmentally 'creative' approach. The time allotted to creative writing, as to teaching reading, seems likely to diminish.[5]

The Cox Committee, like Bullock, did not look at 'A' levels. The Bullock Committee had decided itself to limit its brief by not looking at post-16 education and higher education but did insert one comment: 'We believe that the post-"O" level English syllabus should contain a language element for all pupils who wish to opt for it, and we recommend that "A" level, or whatever examination may replace it, should include a paper on this basis' (11.40). The traditional literature-based syllabus was and is felt to be wanting,[6] even by those students intending to study literature at university and certainly by those who did not intend to take the subject further. The research study by Barnes and Barnes noted in 1984 that students at 'A' level – 'virtually a woman's world' (p. 260) – had less part in interpreting the texts studied than they did in the fifth year (p. 395). The researchers do not link these findings with their own suggestion that pupils can only take charge of the curriculum by classroom intervention (p. 386). Such a linkage might have implications in terms of the gender split at 16 since girls are known to interrupt teachers less often. It will be interesting to see if the number of male students increases with the growth in language courses.

These alternative 'A' level courses involving the student writing in various modes and/or including a language element are flourishing.[7] The schooling offered to 16–18-year-olds is likely to undergo radical changes in the future since it has been left unchanged for many years. Much will depend on the kind of assessment determined on. Nevertheless the form of the 'A' level or its replacement will affect what happens in HE. Students will enter HE with a different set of skills, a diminishing background knowledge of the traditional literary canon and therefore different expectations.

Community writing

'Creative' writing has also flourished (sometimes even by that name) in the last few decades in community groups, access courses and adult literacy courses as well as week and day courses in writing centres often distinctively designed just for writing. Upon occasion this writing has been connected with work in oral history so that communities as well as individuals have been enabled to find a 'published' voice, frequently for the first time. These courses have been so popular and effective that some enthusiasts have described their growth as a 'movement'. As educational ventures they have had to struggle for funds, as continuing education courses usually do, and also have had to struggle to gain respect from the arts establishment. What the community work has achieved above all is a much wider publication rate than ever existed before. New printing processes enabled individuals and groups of writers to see their work published to a high commercial standard.

It is difficult to say what effect these courses have had and will have on the school curriculum. The workshop approach and peer group comment are two significant features which have been recognized in HE courses, as other chapters indicate. Such approaches are more difficult to organize within schools with a National Curriculum to manage and classes of 30 pupils and more. However, if 'pupils should increasingly make their own decisions about their writing – what it is about, what form it should take and to whom it is addressed . . .' (Cox, 17.17), the workshop approach in groups within a class may well be essential to achieve this aim.

Craft and technology

The recent pedagogical emphasis on the process of writing as opposed to the production of a piece of writing has occurred as a result of research, a pragmatic desire to see a child improve one item of written work before moving on to yet another and the advent of new technology. The word 'craft' has figured highly as this emphasis has grown in favour. Stressing the craft involved in the practice of writing has the strategic effect of presenting creative writing as a task, laudably accomplished if worked at. The notion of crafting also fits in, generally speaking, with the comments from professional writers on the way they work. Many universities and HE institutions have had writers in residence and a number of writers have worked within the 'Writers in Schools' programme, both funded in varying degrees by the Arts Council. Published interviews with writers have proliferated in journals of all kinds. This has given an airing to the whole area of writing, the necessity for deletion and redrafting as well as the difficulties of publication. The fact that so many professional writers are now interviewed on their particular way of writing must be due, to some extent, to the increasing interest in writing within the community as well as within schools. Discussion of the hard graft writers engage in is successful ammunition against the notion of spontaneous, free-association, stimulus-driven pieces of undisciplined prose posing as poetry some critics seem to feel is the inevitable outcome of creative writing courses.

At the same time as this growth of interest in the process of writing occurred the use of word processors became more widespread. It may well seem, in 50 years' time or so, that this technology brought about the emphasis on redrafting in English teaching, rather in the way it is claimed that the invention of the stirrup brought in feudalism. This does not seem to be the case in this country, though it is clear that word processors help tremendously. Very young children can add to or alter their writing very easily and, later on, school pupils can redraft for general improvement. They can also see how a piece sounds written in the first person rather than the third, or written as a play not a short story. With the best will in the world *and* a number of highly committed students the amount of redrafting of handwritten work cannot be very great. Comparatively easy redrafting allows writers the confidence to be more objective about their own writing. They can keep a number of drafts and refer back to them if necessary.

The various GCSE Examination Boards did not accept the use of simple word processors in any straightforward manner. They disagreed among themselves as to whether any pieces should be allowed in word-processed form or how many.[8] Conflicting regulations were frustrating for pupils and teachers. Word-processed material and its clearer presentation can also cause problems as regards marking. It seems likely that we tend to give poorer scripts a better mark when we can actually read them.[9]

Apart from the comparatively simple facilitation of redrafting, retention of the drafts for comparison, and 'cut and paste' techniques offered by the word processor, the development of computers inevitably leads on to further possibilities. The likelihood of actual collaborative writing becomes more possible, beyond any basic advice with editing and redrafting. At the least contentious level, for instance, students can help each other with their writing. In my second-year class one student was having trouble writing the end of her documentary. She typed in the version she had written which was networked to other computers. This procedure could also have been accomplished with discs and stand-alone computers. Other students reworked her version as they saw fit. The student then took away eight other versions of the ending, which she said proved very helpful. Such work is still presumably within the domain of advice, though there would be a degree of further collaboration if she had used virtually all of a particular version written by another student.

Collaborative writing has been encouraged in schools, partly, I suspect, owing to the scarcity of computers. It does, however, become much more feasible with the ease of access to one another's scripts. Many writers do work collaboratively (this book is one example) although the relationship in creative writing tends to be that of editor or mentor and writer, for example Ezra Pound and T.S. Eliot. The various novels produced by more than one writer have tended to be experimental so far but it would seem that team productions are very possible in the future. It would be a pity if assessment procedures so far based so centrally on individualistic performance should preclude collaboration. Theatre arts and drama courses are already prepared to assess group projects and there is no reason why writing courses should not do the same.

Writers are becoming used to using word processors at different stages: for compiling notes and ideas, to use a thesaurus, to help undo a writer's block (it is claimed it is easier to 'just write' on a computer than to use a pen or pencil, particularly if the screen brightness is turned so low that the writing is 'invisible'), to redraft either for improvement or variation or even just for presentation purposes. There is some evidence offered that using a word processor heightens the sense of audience.[10] It certainly makes the process of writing quite obvious, though such use heightens the perennial problem of never finishing. The work can always be altered. This 'problem' can also be a benefit, since it helps students realize that a publication date, rather like a performance, is only a date and not necessarily a conclusion.

The new, more powerful computers and their ability to incorporate other media, such as video, may lead to new forms of writing and give encouragement to associative ways of thinking. Hypertext, a computerized cross-referencing system, in particular may lead to new forms or, in a way, return us to old forms. Daniel Chandler, as long ago as 1985,[11] drew up a table in which he compared 'MS and early print culture' with 'the spread of literacy' within what he called a 'networked society'. He decided we were reaching the end of the age of print and its effects – individual authorship, copyright, definitive texts, concept of plagiarism, private, silent reading – and moving towards (or in some instances, backwards) to collaborative works, with no copyright, participatory reading, changeable texts and with writers as publishers.

With programs such as *Hypercard* on Macintosh and *Guide* on IBM computers writers can produce packages of text where the reader may move at will along a number of pathways. By clicking on specific items of text or icons or even parts of a picture the reader/viewer can move to another section. So, for example, a student's portfolio of work might include notes, interview material, illustrations, perhaps a section of another writer's work which is particularly relevant, as well as the original writing. This would be linked in appropriate ways, rather than all put together as a collection in a loose-leaf binder. Such packages will of course be equally possible for critical writing.

Interactive fiction has already begun to affect younger readers via versions of adventure games, often with a fair amount of text involved. Rather more interactive fiction has been designed and composed in the United States for older readers but is not widely available in Britain. It is unlikely to have a major impact on the literary scene, in that the majority of readers probably do not want to make decisions about characters' actions, places and specific items. They prefer to rely on the author's ability to manipulate their interest. The addition of visual and auditory effects to written work seems a much more likely occurrence in the future. Also the fact that association pathways may be an important feature in future creative work may be significant as regards what is written. As Stephen Marcus states: 'computer technology is changing the nature of the product as well as the process of decoding and encoding what's on our minds'.[12] He considers the use of hypermedia will affect our ways of writing and will enable people from different cultures and the two sexes to compose in ways more fruitful to their thought processes.

Technology will not remain as it is. A new revolution, perhaps equal in effect to that of print, is under way. It is to be hoped we can be tolerant of the changes it will bring about without too much Luddite opposition. It will undoubtedly bring more of a lasting change than government intervention at the National Curriculum level. However there are other changes already under way in teaching writing in the first years of school as part of a 'whole language' process. This method will in all likelihood gain in prestige throughout the school curriculum. In the past HE has tended not to take note of what is happening at junior school level but it is now time to catch up.

With these great changes in technology and curriculum in progress we need even more to see creative writing exist as a subject area. It is too precious to disappear in a welter of tasks or multi-media 'effects'. I hope it is true, as some people aver, that at least we need no longer apologize for the name or seek another one.

Notes

1 Terry Eagleton, *Literary Theory* (Oxford, Basil Blackwell, 1983) p. 11.
2 Jacqueline Rose, *The Case of Peter Pan, or the Impossibility of Children's Fiction* (London, Macmillan, 1984). See in particular Chapter 5, 'Peter Pan, Language and the State'.
3 Board of Education publications, including annual and departmental reports, memoranda, circulars and pamphlets are most easily accessible at the Library of the Department of Education and Science, London. They are less accessible in the Public Records Office. Individual reports and circulars can be found in various libraries in the UK.
4 John Rae, 'The decline and fall of English grammar', *Observer*, 7 February 1982. I am indebted to my colleague, John Harris, for bringing this quotation to my attention.
5 Fran Abrams, *Times Educational Supplement*, 28 June 1991.
6 D. Barnes and D. Barnes, *Versions of English* (Oxford, Heinemann Educational, 1984); Nicholas Pyke, 'Taken Apart by the Word Processors', *Times Educational Supplement*, 14 June 1991, p. 8.
7 Pyke, ibid.
8 'GCSE English and Wordprocessing', in M. Monteith (ed.) *English and Computing* (Language Development Centre Publication, Sheffield City Polytechnic, 1988) pp. 53–5.
9 Evidence quoted in a research paper given by Mike Peacock at Conference on Language and Computers, Sheffield City Polytechnic, 1989 (to be published in M. Monteith (ed.) *Language and Computers*, Oxford, Intellect Books).

10 Collette Daiute, 'The Computer as Stylus and Audience', *College Composition and Communication* (1983) **34** (2), 134–45.
11 Daniel Chandler, in D. Chandler and S. Marcus (eds) *Computers and Literacy* (Milton Keynes, Open University Press, 1985) p. 3.
12 Stephen Marcus, 'Multimedia, Hypermedia, and the teaching of English' (to be published in M. Monteith (ed.) *Language and Computers*, Intellect Books).

2

The teaching of creative writing

Philip Hobsbaum

I

Those who study a subject should also study its history. English Literature in the universities of Victorian England began as an off-shoot of classics and was taught by professors who were themselves not good enough classicists. It was thought to be second-best, studied by women and foreigners and, as such, has never been deeply respected. The bulk of its students were held to be taking an easy option. Therefore the English course was salted with doses of Anglo-Saxon and philology, to prevent it from losing academic respectability altogether.

In Scotland the process was different. There the study of English evolved from rhetoric, which was itself a branch of logic and which was therefore taught by philosophers. The most notable pioneer was Adam Smith. His lectures in rhetoric, only recently discovered by J.M. Lothian and definitively edited by J.C. Bryce, were the model for all such ventures until well into the 1860s. They exist in the form of a transcript by two anonymous students who attended these lectures in the Glasgow University session 1762–3. Adam Smith's practicality and eye for detail are worthy of remark: 'Perspicuity of stile requires not only that the expressions we use should be free from all ambiguity proceeding from synonimous words but that the words should be natives if I may say so of the language we speak in.'[1] 'Perspicuity' is one of Smith's positive criteria; another is 'propriety'. His pupil, George Jardine, was Professor of Logic from 1787 to 1827. He gave his own version of the Lectures in *Belles Lettres*, still with the aims of perspicuity and propriety well in his sights.[2] Jardine, in his turn, was succeeded by *his* pupil, Robert Buchanan, who was rebuked by a University Commission for setting the Logic Class too much written work. Unrepentantly he recommended that Rhetoric should be set up as a separate course, a view which foreshadowed the institution of English as a subject at Glasgow University.[3] His chosen treatise was *The Philosophy of Rhetoric* by George Campbell, which was concurrently used in Edinburgh and Aberdeen (at which latter university Campbell had been Principal of Marischal College) as well as at Glasgow. Indeed Campbell's book was in use well after the creation of a Chair of English at Glasgow University in 1862. It adduces, with many negative examples, faults familiar to any first-year tutor today, such as the sentence that drags its slow length along through many subjects, losing antecedents for its pronouns in the process.[4] From all this it will be seen that the provenance of English at Scottish universities was quite different from that in England, where the teaching of literature was an off-shoot from classical and, more recently, modern language studies.

Students in England were encouraged to read Shakespeare and Milton as revelations of national character. In Scotland, under the counsel of professors such as John Nichol, the courses were oriented towards composition. Swift and Addison were held up as models of style, and the fact that most students were destined to express themselves through the medium of conceptual prose was never far out of sight. Unfortunately Nichol's successors were A.C. Bradley, Walter Raleigh and W. Macneile Dixon, and they brought patriotic models of English teaching, developed in England, to the formation of honours schools in Scottish universities.[5] The emphasis on composition, in consequence, attenuated. From the publication of Bradley's book, *Shakespearian Tragedy*, literature as taught at Oxford dominated English departments in Scotland.

The dubious nature of English courses in England may be seen in terms of the fate suffered by creative writers who followed them. Auden was given a third class degree and Betjeman was sent down. Only after the Second World War did creativity seem to be recognized as anything other than a liability: both Philip Larkin and Geoffrey Hill obtained firsts in English. Even now, however, the creative writer is a *lusus naturae* on the university staff. Usually allowed only a temporary fellowship, he is likely to find himself patronized and marginalized. One remembers the comparison, made by Randall Jarrell, between a writer at a conference and a pig in a bacon-judging contest: 'Go away, pig! What do you know about bacon?'[6] There are indeed poets, such as F.T. Prince and Donald Davie, who have become professors. But they were not usually appointed because of their poetry. They will be found to have been formidable academics, with an impressive record of efficiency in teaching and administration.

There is surely something lop-sided in this. When one 'teaches' a student 'English Literature', what one is really doing is teaching her to write about it – 'her' because English students tend to be women, although their professors are not. There was an understandable amount of pressure from middle-class women in the later nineteenth century to enter university. Few of them had the classical training of their brothers who had been to public school. So, when at last the doors were opened to them, in the 1880s and 1890s, they tended to opt for modern literary studies. In fact it is impossible to speak of the rise of English Literature, as taught in the universities, without at the same time discussing the higher education of women. Of course they were entering a field dominated by men. Many of them – Virginia Woolf is a notable example – were suspicious not only of the university but of the teaching of literature therein. Much in recent practice shows these suspicions to be soundly based. It has been said that women tend to get degrees inferior in classification to those acquired by men. Women, however, are pursuing courses designed by male academics for male students. There are comparatively few women professors; nothing like the proportion of women studying arts subjects. To that extent the courses are unrepresentative. Were men to study curricula devised by women using techniques designed for women, the results might be quite different. As it is, the shadows of the founding fathers of academic English – Walter Raleigh, Oliver Elton, G.C. Moore-Smith – stretch far. It is true that one teaches students to write about English Literature; in other words, the encouragement of composition is going forward. But it is going forward in a curiously limited way. It is confined to the form of the critical essay.

Now the critical essay is a respectable form. It was utilized by such writers as Dryden, Coleridge, Arnold, James and T.S. Eliot. Yet it is not for their critical essays that they are primarily remembered; not even the author of 'Dover Beach', not even the author of 'Burnt Norton'. A good deal of their critical output, further, is wayward and sometimes even misleading. One would not recommend, without serious qualification, Dryden on Fletcher, Coleridge on Fielding, or Arnold on Tolstoy; still less, Eliot on the novel.

If celebrities such as these undergo lapses in using the form of the critical essay, what chance have our students? To put the question another way, who are the great English critics – apart, that is, from the writers already named? One would certainly include Johnson; one might include Hazlitt; in the twentieth century, with F.A. Leavis, Wilson Knight and Yvor Winters as possible nominees, consensus would seem to go out of the window. If there are a dozen critics writing in English about whose distinction a group of modern academics could agree, it would be surprising. The inference is that there are fewer good critics than good writers and that criticism is therefore a hard practice to follow.

Yet thousands upon thousands of students come up to British universities, and many more to those in the United States, to be taught criticism. It would be easier to teach them to write poems, or stories or plays. In those genres there are more examples of efficacy and, in judging them, a greater incidence of consensus. But, for reasons that are never argued out, the teaching of creative writing is held not to be academically respectable. This does not seem to be the case with the music departments, where composition is an essential part of the course. Why then should it be thought in some degree fraudulent when one comes to English?

It could be argued that we have no hope of turning out a Shakespeare. But what music department is geared to produce a Mozart? A music department exists to teach basic skills, such as counterpoint, harmony and orchestration. Such basic skills are the responsibility of English departments also: syntax, bibliophily, the construction of essays. These are matters of craft; that fine poet, Seamus Heaney, called these skills 'the craft... of making. It wins competitions in the *Irish Times* or the *New Statesman*'. Technique, he goes on to say, 'technique entails... the whole creative effort of the mind's and body's resources to bring the meaning of experience within the jurisdiction of form'.[7] One probably cannot teach technique; it is a matter of the creative writer defining her own self in relation to her context. But she is not going to be able to do this unless she has learned her craft. She will have to take note of Robert Lowell, whose *Life Studies*, based on his unbearable family,[8] might have collapsed into the hysteria characteristic of so many confessional poets if he had not studied craft under a series of masters: Richard Eberhart, John Crowe Ransom, Allen Tate, Randall Jarrell; the last, his near contemporary but, none the less, his master.

The concept of apprenticeship, manifest in music, architecture and painting, has either not existed or has been lost when it comes to literature. One does not apprentice oneself to a Ransom or a Jarrell; one just happens to go to the local university, or the one one's father went to, or one with a pleasant river or trendy social life. Once there, one finds that, in so far as creative writing is taught, it is taught by a poet or playwright penuriously subsisting on a minimal stipend for a couple of years if he or she is lucky, less if he or she happens to get on the wrong side of the staff.

What has happened is that English Literature has got itself trapped in a time-warp. Because philology was deemed essential to the study of classics it has formed a notable part of English studies. Yet an equally important sector of classics, the writing of Greek and Latin verse and prose, has never acclimatized in an adapted form to academic English. There has never been in this century, so far as Great Britain is concerned, a serious attempt to teach composition. This may be because writing in a dead language was deemed to be a technique, while writing in a living vernacular might bring in personal emotions. This is to ignore the fact that a great deal of one's sensibility is involved in writing that which students are expected to write: literary criticism.

This suggests that it is the university staff that matter; not the students. The staff have been taught in a certain way, historical intentionalism at Oxford, the New Criticism at Cambridge, and they will perpetuate their education without development; without, even, knowing the history of the subject they profess to teach. They will teach literary criticism, but they will not necessarily know why. It has always been so, in their short lifetime, and therefore so it must always be.

What if one challenges this arbitrary state of affairs and proposes that criticism be relegated to an ancillary, and perhaps optional, area in our courses? What if one proposes courses in writing fiction; writing poetry; writing plays, even? The first response would most likely be to say that the present university staff is not qualified to judge such efforts; after all, 'how can we judge literature until it is embalmed in history?' – the actual words of a Scottish academic, now holding a chair in the Antipodes. Many more academics of this cast of mind – notice the implications of the metaphor 'embalmed' – and we might as well abandon literature to the mausoleum. If it is true that our present teaching of English literature cannot judge contemporary work, how can we judge the topics of the past, or the critical essays our students produce on those topics? But we must not be seduced into flaccid conformity: it is not Shakespeare or Milton we are seeking to teach, but those capable of appreciating Shakespeare or Milton. To understand Mozart it is not necessary to write as well as Mozart, or there would be no music students at all.

If it is true that we have no academics capable of teaching composition, then we should set about acquiring some. In the past we have kept our appointments system rigid: no graduate has a hope of teaching literature in a university context without a first in English – which, remember, means a first in literary criticism. This prime qualification is irrelevant even to the teaching of literary criticism. F.R. Leavis got a poor second in history; Wilson Knight a poor second in English; A.P. Blackmur got no degree at all. Mighty figures of the past are also poorly qualified: Wordsworth received only a pass degree, and Coleridge dropped out. It seems that, to be a great critic, you do not need to succeed in writing criticism, at least as an undergraduate; only those who teach the subject need to do so.

Dryden and Arnold were, of course, not qualified in English. What can we deduce from that? Surely that a good book, the production of a distinguished text, is the ultimate qualification. Geoffrey Hill was qualified by his first to be a university lecturer; so was Edwin Morgan. But is not Hill's *For the Unfallen* still more of a qualification; is not Morgan's *A Second Life*? If writing some of the best poetry of our time does not qualify the author to teach literature, what can qualify that author?

It may be said – it *was* said, in conversation, by the classical scholar, Michael Grant – that appointing writers is a risky business; you don't know how they'll turn out. Well, Geoffrey Hill and Edwin Morgan seem to have turned out pretty well, and there are many who have been on appointments committees and seen *their* academic candidates turn out for the worse. Universities are no more immune than factories, offices or organs of the media to incursions of crooks, drunkards and drones. They survive, as other organizations do, through the efforts of those others, who are doing the work.

It may be argued that we cannot employ people who have graduated in another subject or those, like R.P. Blackmur and Ian Fletcher, who have not graduated at all. This is a legalistic point and most universities possess calendars that a competent lawyer could fault in a hundred particulars. In fact, though, there is no problem with regard to qualifications: any university has the power to confer a degree upon whomsoever its senate chooses. This is not a matter of degrees that are honorary. The university by act of senate can confer upon an architect whom it wishes to employ a degree, should he have none of his own, that will enable him to teach architecture. Why should this be not true of writers? It would not necessarily have to be a first degree. A doctorate is a higher degree which declares one can teach. There is such a thing in the calendar as a D.Litt. – real, not honorary, and conferred in respect of published work. Most universities keep this degree, which at present is under-utilized, for their own graduates or for members of their staff, but there is every reason why the ordinance should be extended. Why not appoint Alasdair Gray or Jim Kelman as professors of literature and qualify them by conferring on them their own doctorates?

The answer is that neither Alasdair Gray nor Jim Kelman wish to teach in a university. They might think that the climate would be hostile to them. Nobody, however, implies that they *could not* teach if they chose. After all, they have done distinguished work as Writing Fellows. How could it be worse for them to be established as permanent members of staff, to have tenure and develop long-term projects, if that is indeed what tenure entails? In any case, if applications for writing fellowships are anything to go by, there are enough writers willing to teach without conscripting others into service. Many of these cannot be lecturers because of the restrictive practices so far followed by the universities. Those have, in their turn, unduly restricted our courses. The answer is to widen the courses. We do not need to exclude criticism, if criticism is indeed what our students wish to write. We should not, either, exclude the possibility of their learning the craft of poetry, or the craft of fiction, or the craft of drama. Such studies would not prevent students from reading literary texts; practical engagement could only enhance their appreciation. This activity would lay down the foundation of good reading for many and good writing for those prepared to develop their craft into a technique.

II

At this juncture the mask of impersonality should be laid aside in order to permit practical considerations to follow. I have been responsible for the management of four writing groups, respectively in Cambridge, London, Belfast and Glasgow. What follows is some indication of the inception and development of the group in London.

The Cambridge Group, formed in 1952 when I was an undergraduate, had moved from a concern mainly with verse speaking to becoming a forum for young writers. One characteristic persisted from Cambridge to the more important off-shoot that was to evolve in London. Acting upon a suggestion from one of my teachers, H.A. Mason, I typed out the poems or stories that were to be read at each meeting and sent copies to the regular clientele beforehand. This made for a concentration on the text rather than considerations less relevant. The poet Peter Redgrove dominated the Cambridge Group, physically as well as intellectually, and it was very much at Redgrove's instigation that I started, in October 1955, a London version of the group. Because of the larger numbers of people involved, the secretarial side became increasingly complicated. I was fortunate to have as group secretary my then fiancée, Hannah Kelly, whose ability to produce accurate stencils meant that people received comely prints rather than the smudged carbon copies they had endured at Cambridge.

The London Group expanded as I spotted incipient writers likely to take an interest in our proceedings, and as participants recommended their friends. One of the originators of the London Group was Julian Cooper, an Argentinian poet I had known at Cambridge, now a documentary film director. Talented writer though he proved to be, his most crucial contribution to the group was bringing along a young bookshop assistant, Peter Porter, now recognized as one of the most distinguished poets in Britain as well as in his native Australia. Peter Redgrove introduced his neighbour, the late Martin Bell, whom he had met in front of the poetry section in his local library. Edward Lucie-Smith, sometimes credited with founding the London Group, did not in fact join us until five months after we had started, on completing his National Service in the RAF. Formidably articulate, Lucie-Smith brought to bear the talents of an analytical critic – he is now mainly known for his work in art reviewing – not only on our work but on his own, exquisitely turned, poems. The subversive tactics of Martin Bell and others sometimes pushed him towards literary stances more reactionary than any he would have chosen for himself. Under much the same pressure, though my strategy was different, I usually let the discussion polarize to some extent before intervening. It was a matter of avoiding closure. I did not wish to use my position as chairman to inhibit discussion by laying down a firm line early in the meeting.

From 1957 onwards I took down the discussion on a tape recorder. The group met on Fridays, and I spent my Saturday mornings studying the divergencies that had arisen the evening before. What seemed to me to distinguish these from the kind of criticism that usually got disseminated in print was the high degree of concentration on verbal detail. This was a direct result of circulating copies of the work that was the subject of discussion to participants beforehand. Psycho-biographizing and triflings with exordia, characteristics one found in even quite respectable causeries, had no place here.

At this point I had better cite an example. The author of the text that occasioned the following discussion was George MacBeth. If he does not quite live up to his reputation as an articulate broadcaster, that is because a convention had grown requiring the author to speak as little as possible. The other people present included Martin Bell, Peter Porter and Christopher Hampton – the political apologist, not the playwright.

Poem in a Metre of Ernest Dowson
Somewhere (yes, I know where,
No, I won't tell you where)
Well-fed, warm and at ease
Lying late in a bed
Out of a window I
Watch a dead station-wall.
Scene one: nothing, as yet.

Next, through wet streets I walk,
Rinsed out after the rain,
Someone (no, I don't know
Who, but only her – yes)
Walks in front of me, well
Wrapped up after the rain.
Scene two: all right, you win.

Somehow (well, you know how,
You've been there in your time)
Women's fingers that lock
Lock and lock and lock. Well,
The upstairs to a room
Bang up against a wall.
Scene three: back as you were.

Scene four (is there a fourth?
No, it just peters out).
Why does every affair
Sometimes (looking around
One's life) seem to involve
Just the same station wall
Seen from bed in the rain?

PORTER: Well, let me put myself on record as saying I thought it was an extremely good poem, but I don't think I quite understood it.
BELL: Do you mean that you're torn between two conflicting interpretations?
PORTER: No, I'm not torn between two conflicting interpretations. Just one, and I don't think I know what it is.
HAMPTON: I think it's possible to have a good poem that one doesn't understand – quite easily.

PORTER: Actually, it's not a good thing. It's not only me, I mean. What I mean is that what I don't understand I take to be me and not the poem. It has that sort of feeling. It has a quality of poetry about it which I'm not at all sure if I feel. If I can't understand it, it probably is me, in this case.

BELL: I'm not entirely sure in verse 3 whether the woman is in the room as well as the poet or not.

PORTER: I should hope so!

MACBETH: Anyone else feel that difficulty?

PORTER: It's the little summing-ups at the end of each stanza which I find uncomfortable.

HAMPTON: I didn't read it like that, Martin, I must admit.

MACBETH: Like what?

HAMPTON: With the woman in the room.

BELL: All those women's fingers that lock, lock, lock . . . this is a fairly strong sequence.

PORTER: So's the second one. I'd almost welcome – it's a most unfair thing to ask for a gloss to a certain extent.

HOBSBAUM: Mind you, here I don't see the difficulty, actually . . . I think, really, it's trying to show something which might have been meaningful and is actually meaningless – and I think that the clue surely is 'why does every affair sometimes . . .' and the word *petering* out – it is nothing anyway, a pointless affair. Being a narrative, he deliberately says Scene 1 nothing's happened; Scene 2 nothing's about to happen; Scene 3, nothing *appears* to be happening; at the end, Scene 4, no, it just peters out. Nothing's happened at all because there has been nothing terribly involved within it – that's what I get from it – there may be more than that.

BELL: You are saying, if you get that final meaning you could treat the rest as a kind of algebraical formula where the A or B could mean variable things, and you'd still get the same conclusion in the last stanza. Either there could be an *actual* affair which peters out or just a *fancied* one that peters out. Both readings would go right through.

HOBSBAUM: Yes, except that I don't think the end would have the same force if it was a fancied one – there wouldn't be any reason for that kind of weariness setting in in the last stanza.

PORTER: No reason for a *phantom* affair to end up or seem to involve just the same station seen from bed in the rain.

HOBSBAUM: Surely it is an action without love, or without any kind of feeling at all, really.

It seems to me now, some 30 years after the event, that the poem is about an encounter that did not take place. Indeed the failure of that encounter to take place is the point of the poem. Of course this reading could be disputed. But that, surely, is what discussion is about. In the London Group nobody pronounced from on high. We did not go in for gurus.

The principle we observed in this group was maintained in other groups I helped to form in Belfast and in Glasgow. Scripts were distributed beforehand, so that group discussion tended outwards from the words on the page, rather than moving peripherally through biography, intention or even less relevant backchat.

This is not the only approach in teaching creative writing, obviously. Not all writers are 'group' people. But there is no doubt in my mind that, for most writers, isolation is harmful, and that contact with an alert audience can only be beneficial. It is very important that all members of a group should be active participants, contributing work, whatever its nature, for discussion in due course. It is important, too, that the comment should be multifarious, including, so far as possible, everyone present. The job of the chairman is to indicate areas of discussion, not to act as final judge or arbiter. The process is a matter of using the individual's capacity to help himself or herself; a mode of encouraging both skill and self-criticism. This is not directed towards revising the text under discussion, though revision has been known to take place as a result of group discussion. Rather it is a means of preparing the ground for the text to come.

Notes

1 Adam Smith, *Lectures on Rhetoric and Belles Lettres,* ed. J.C. Bryce (Oxford, Clarendon Press, 1983) Lecture 2.
2 George Jardine, *Synopsis of Lectures on Logic and Belles Lettres* (Glasgow, 1913).
3 *Minutes of Evidence . . . taken and received by the Commissioners reappointed by William IV . . . for Visiting the Universities of Scotland* (London, 1837) Vol. II: Buchanan's Testimony, pp. 36–42.
4 George Campbell, *The Philosophy of Rhetoric* (Edinburgh, 1776) Book II, Chapter 6.
5 The report of the Government Department of Education committee on *The Teaching of English in England* (London, HMSO, 1921); George Sampson, *English for the English* (Cambridge, CUP, 1921); W. Macneile Dixon, *Poetry and National Character* (Cambridge, CUP, 1915).
6 Randall Jarrell, *Poetry and the Age* (London, Faber and Faber, 1955, rep. 1973) p. 74.
7 Seamus Heaney, *Preoccupations: Selected Prose 1969–78* (London, Faber and Faber, 1980) p. 87.
8 Robert Lowell, *Life Studies* (London, Faber and Faber, 1959).

3

Creative writing, contemporary theory and the English curriculum

Robert Miles

Considered as an integral part of English studies, creative writing has fared less well in England than it has in North America. Several mutually reinforcing factors seem responsible for this difference: the North American four-year degree provides greater latitude for the provision of marginal courses than the more specialized and streamlined English three-year degree; course-planning in America is, comparatively, less trammelled; the North American academy has played a larger role as patron to the contemporary writer; and, finally, the demands of the academic consumer have been different. As Janet Burroway argues elsewhere in this book, an upshot of the American system of mass education at a tertiary level has been, in departments of literature, the presence of students who, lacking a literary background, find practice rather than analysis a more conducive route to literary appreciation.

But English, in England, is at present in a state of flux, as hardly needs saying. Pressures for change are being exerted from within and without, from above and below. The demand to expand provision without a corresponding increase in resources has turned attention to the 'mass' system of North America, to see what lessons can be learned from modularization and semesters. The Core Curriculum and new 'A' level syllabuses may possibly choke the supply of fine-tuned specialists primed for a three-year sprint (by reducing curricular time while reaching out to the non-specialist). The canon itself has begun to fragment as the curriculum attempts to reach 'down' to students traditionally by-passed by HE and outwards across a multi-cultural nation. And, of course, the canon has been put under intense scrutiny within the subject itself. Here I think it true to say that contemporary theory has been the instrument rather than the cause of this fragmenting scrutiny. Where consensus once was, difference now is.

Institutional changes and the redrawing of curricular boundaries offer creative writing an opportunity to move in from the margins. Contemporary theory has helped thaw once rigid demarcations; if the recommendations of the Cox Report pass from theory to practice, creative writing will increasingly have a pre-degree life; and as the system becomes more flexible there will be more scope to respond to student demand for writing.

In this chapter I intend to explore the relationship between contemporary theory and creative writing. I want to show how contemporary theory has altered the perception of creative writing, but also how creative writing offers perspectives on contemporary theory. In particular I want to argue not only that the tendency of contemporary theory to question boundaries and demarcations undoes the unhelpful categorization of practice versus analysis, vocational versus academic, creative writing versus English, but that creative writing can helpfully, and rigorously, question contemporary theory. To put it another way, 'contemporary' theory helps bring out what is uncompromisingly hard in so-called 'soft' creative writing, while creative writing in turn helps bring out the disconcertingly soft in hard theory. I have started this chapter with a reminder of institutional differences and changes because I want to ground my discussion in the practical and possible. Within the institution creative writing must be regarded as part of a curriculum bounded by historical constraints even as that curriculum is reshaped by new pressures. The three-year degree is perhaps the most significant constraint. The significance here is that, given this tight frame, creative writing cannot afford to be thought of as a tasty extra, but must make a case for being part of the curricular structure. I intend to set out a case within the context of the shifting boundaries mentioned above.

To begin with, creative writing finds itself paradoxically situated in relation to contemporary theory. By 'contemporary theory' I largely mean that theoretical impetus that has begun to nudge English into a more capacious field of critical enquiry often denominated 'cultural studies'. In recent years there has been something of a paradigm shift, to cultural studies, and away from an older disciplinary model I shall associate with New Criticism for the sake of argumentative convenience. To simplify further, the New Critical paradigm may be said to have combined two elements: (1) a canon of texts commonly agreed to embody aesthetic excellence and (2) established protocols for their non-reductive analysis, for bringing out what is unique in each text. The critical paradigm of contemporary theory is different on both counts. Once again one begins with a body of texts, but this time the selection is, ostensibly, non-evaluative. And instead of a series of transmissible protocols teasing out the unique, one encounters a set of, on the whole, complementary theories locating typical differences – complementary because these theories agree in formulating the critical act as one that 'reads' through the text to a cultural context that conditions, and therefore imparts meaning to, the text. This is true of even so-called 'deconstructive' theory which, once the dust settles, tends to situate its analytic manoeuvres within contemporaneous, and therefore culturally inflected, rhetoric. One can also see this cultural paradigm at work in psychoanalytic criticism. Whereas Freudian criticism might have been used to establish what was *sui generis* in a work through a linkage with the peculiar psyche that produced it, modern psychoanalytic criticism is more likely to be employed as a means of articulating the acculturated deep structures that link one text with another. To call a work 'phallocentric' is only understood to have meaning if other similarly situated texts can also be established as phallocentric: it draws attention to something ineluctable in their condition.

The tendency of contemporary theory, then, is for 'culture' to replace the text as the primary object of study. As the mystique of the text fades, so, too, do the customary lines of division, between the literary and the non-literary, the canonical and the popular, now transliterated as questions of gender, race and class. Thus autobiography, diaries, travel writing, graffiti, even criticism, all become legitimate objects of study.

Given this post-modern celebration of multiplicity and diversity, creative writing, in wanting to join the party, will naturally find itself pushing against an open door, except that, in doing so, it may very well find itself appearing as the ghost at the feast or, to use a theoretical figure, as the return of the repressed. Contemporary theory not only decentres the object of study, from text to context, but also from 'author' to the cultural energies that make his or her text possible. Creative writing, on the face of it, replaces the author in her/his accustomed, privileged position as the mind at the centre of the text. But on top of this it is saddled with an additional image, that of creativity, inspiration, or Romantic genius. The casual discourse of creative writing at best reinstates the language of intention – people ask what the writer did or meant – and at worst reinvites gush about the transcendental subject. Even the studious middle course – of talking resolutely about craft – offers mechanics where contemporary theory has in mind more abstruse means of cultural transmission.

I have deliberately represented creative writing in a light most teachers of it will recognize as clichéd travesty of what actually happens in practice. I have done so partly as a first step in reversing this misperception, but partly because I want to keep in focus the contradictory pull between the tendencies of contemporary theory and the drift of creative writing. As I shall argue, there is an overlap, a consonance of purpose between them, but there is also this tension: contemporary theory's erosion of the traditional boundaries of the discipline invites creative writing in, but creative writing appears to reinstate the very primacy of the subject contemporary theory actively demotes. I believe that at bottom there is an irreducible tension between the manoeuvres of contemporary theory and the practice of teaching creative writing. This conflict, what one might call a 'tensed complementariness', from the point of view of a healthy curriculum is, I believe, pedagogically, both useful and necessary.

Earlier I made the point that the establishment of creative writing within the curriculum necessarily takes place within institutional constraints, and that it was undesirable simply to inject creative writing, as if it were some kind of supercharged syllabus. One has to think about curricular theory, about what it is that separates a vocational course from an academic one, the acquisition of skills from intellectual inquiry. In science the verification of hypotheses (the principle of falsifiability together with practices capable of distinguishing the false) is a distinguishing feature of the academic curriculum; but in an arts course this principle is replaced by a dialectic between theory and practice, between the projected fit a theory construes and the concrete particularity of the object itself. In applying a Laconian reading, say, one asks whether the application benefits the text, whether the work is adequately covered by it, or whether there is an uncomfortable surplus that threatens to invalidate the reading. The notion that no single reading is ever complete is different from the question of whether a particular reading fits or works. The first reflects a principle of disciplinarity (if readings were complete the subject would decay into the transmission of facts) whereas the second is a question we bring to bear in the assessment of the success of a particular instance.

The tension I have sketched above, between the theoretical orientation of the cultural studies paradigm and the practical nuance of creative writing, brings just such curricular benefits, satisfies just such dialectical demands. At its simplest it affords the student the opportunity of comparing theories of how texts come into being with the actual experience of bringing texts into being. But this tension may also feed into creative writing more directly.

There are two ways of articulating the relevant, polar positions. It is the conflict between regarding writing from the point of view of the professional writer, of those producing writing for a market-place, on the one side and, on the other, regarding texts from the vantage-point of literary criticism. It is also the difference between teaching writing as a verbal art and regarding writing from the viewpoint of critical studies.

These two conflicts are similar, but not identical. To teach writing as a verbal art immediately invites parallels with 'vocational' art courses, such as film, drama, painting, sculpture and, perhaps, to a lesser extent, music. Here three elements assume an importance: an appreciation of the history of the craft; a mastery of its techniques; and an inquiry into the contemporary, into what is vital, or viable, and what is not, into what constitutes 'saying something, now', and what is simply derivative.

I can best address the other conflict by giving an illustration. The literary studies degree on which I teach, which has a compulsory creative writing syllabus, frequently throws up a situation in which a student will wish to write in a formulaic genre, such as science fiction. Those, like myself, whose orientation arises from their 'traditional' position within literary studies are most likely to ask the student to make some kind of critical inquiry into their choice of genre, so that they think about what it is the genre says, how it says it, and why they feel it necessary to say it in that way. But the degree is also home to professional writers, temporarily resident. Professional writers are likely to be far less patient with formula writing; the imperative under which they work, to engage with 'real writing', with voices that are somehow vital, generally leads to an insistence that the student break out of the safe, the derivative, the unoriginal. For the academic teacher of writing, the critical may take precedence. Late in life, when he feared his failing powers might degenerate into senility, Dr Johnson reported to Boswell that he had the night before written a bad poem. Johnson felt he was OK as long as he knew his poems were bad. Similarly it may be considered unimportant if students write badly, so long as they know they have, and that they know, critically, what the difference is. But writers in their own professional lives live under a burden of creativity, a burden under which they see all writing taking place. The discipline professional writers place on their students often leads to student complaints that the writer wants to make them write like her or him. But usually this is only to say that the writer has painfully worked her or himself to what feels to them the leading edge, and that they want to help their students, if not to get there themselves, then to see what that place looks like.

These two related conflicts, then, are also curricular matters. The tension modifies as one introduces theory into a verbal arts degree, or verbal arts into critical studies, setting theoreticians among practitioners, or practitioners among theoreticians. At this juncture my essay branches off in the direction of the latter, of fitting creative writing into traditional English. I do not mean to suggest that a verbal arts degree is less or more viable than a literary studies one, or that the tension between theory and practice is any less relevant to it. But one has to keep in mind that there are fundamental curricular differences. Perhaps the most obvious way of bringing them out is to remind ourselves that a verbal arts degree would presumably have aspiring, experienced writers as its student body, whereas a literary studies degree has experienced and aspiring critics. A verbal arts degree would be a more radical departure from the curricular status quo, but my immediate aim is the more limited one of making a case for verbal arts, for finding a legitimate curricular space for creative writing within the changing landscape of the degree in literary studies. And here I see the main task as one of establishing the academic legitimacy for doing so, to counteract the common view that, however much creative writing may nurture the unconscious, it does little to help a student's critical and theoretical awareness.

But here one is confronted by some hard, curricular choices. As mentioned earlier, simply to 'bolt on' a creative writing component is not a compelling option. Given a four-year degree, a free-floating creative writing syllabus, which may or may not feed into students' critical experience, looks an inexpensive luxury. But within the context of a three-year degree that is expanding access, with a changing clientele and 'A' level, it may seem very expensive indeed. And this is especially true given the changes within the subject. The cultural studies paradigm expects not less knowledge but more. For instance, one can hardly expect students to tackle the cultural significance of generic change without a wide knowledge of both the genre and the culture in which it changes. In the present circumstances curricular development is like stowing gear in a small boat: everything has to be arranged with strict economy.

If creative writing is introduced in a literary degree, then, it must earn its curricular keep. To be sure, from the point of view of educational 'consumers', there is a buoyant demand for creative writing, but so is there for feminist studies, or film. The demand needs to be translated into an educationally compelling shape.

Within a literary studies degree, if creative writing is to be added, something, somewhere, must give. As my earlier opposition of the two paradigms, cultural studies and New Criticism, suggests, the obvious curricular strand for excision is practical criticism. Contemporary theory's discontent with New Criticism sometimes expresses itself in shifts of nomenclature, sometimes method, from, say, 'prac. crit.' to 'close reading', or to 'stylistics'. The substitution of creative writing for practical criticism would not mean the abandonment of close reading, but a more practical institution of it. The first part of my case for this substitution is that creative writing efficiently promotes skills of close reading while being in consonance with the curricular changes triggered by contemporary theory.

Part of the argument against practical criticism was that it encoded a congeries of related literary values and procedures always in need of corrective defamiliarization by theory. Creative writing also has its congeries. One is not simply swapping equivalent methods. The difference between practical criticism and creative writing enounces itself as early as the seminar. The creative writing seminar will have an agenda and a set of protocols. Say we are dealing with a second-year prose workshop, with students who have already had experience in the craft of writing stories. The agenda may be a 'naturalistic' story (in the loose sense of the term). After looking at examples, say a story by Sherwood Anderson, or one from *The Dubliners*, the students are asked to write, in class, the opening paragraph of their own naturalistic story (a helpful and often rewarding variation here may be to agree collectively on the story line first: this gets over the immediate problem of invention while offering the opportunity of comparing treatments). Or it may happen that the student decides to write a naturalistic story for their folder of submitted works and brings it to the seminar for discussion. It will then be photocopied and distributed. Here two protocols (in my experience, crucially necessary ones) come into play: the student must read out their work, and then must remain silent until the class collectively invites comment.

As in the course of any teaching, matters at this juncture may fail dismally:

the class may remain stonily silent until the exasperated tutor pronounces. Success, on the other hand, will arise from the peculiar nature of the creative writing seminar. It is a *sine qua non* of good teaching that the tutor be sensitive to group dynamics. Again seminars work best when there is a collective sense of purpose, of being part of a common project. Students must feel that the agenda is one within their competence, something in which they have a legitimate say, and grounds for saying it. A familiar criticism levelled at practical criticism was that it found itself shrouded in the aura of a priestly craft: the initiate patiently learned from the tutor/master, dazzled by arcane skills. In my experience a creative writing seminar is less likely to experience this disengagement. Say the student producing the naturalistic story, as frequently happens, ends their work by saying too much, by closing their story, falling into telling rather than showing. The members of the seminar will find themselves involved on several levels: the group, collectively, comes to a view; each individual is involved in a similar project; each member has invested their own sensitivities in their work. All three levels of involvement will come into play as the group decides whether or not the ending works. At the same time, because it is their own work, creative writing raises in an acute form the issues of authority and ownership. The level of involvement inhering within creative writing spurs a group bonding, creating a dynamic, while the issue of authority gives it an edge.

Of course matters are seldom as blandly utopian as that. The seminar, out of deference, shyness, hesitation, or group bonding itself, may simply approve, inducing the tutor to make the critical running on the aesthetic inadvisability of closure. In my experience it is here that the creative writing seminar's difference valuably comes into being. No matter how tentatively presented, in a literature seminar the tutor's comments are likely to be absorbed as simply authoritative, but in a creative writing seminar members will frequently group together in vigorous defence of their colleague, challenging the tutor's authority, protecting their involvement, their right to judge. Such conflict, it seems to me, is the basis of learning in the arts. The question is not whether students come to a correct view, but whether they energetically enter the process of forming a view; and here willingness to challenge the tutor is essential. The creative writing seminar, with its sense of a shared project and personal investment, fosters this willingness.

Although such conflict inheres within the creative writing seminar, it also requires nurture and an appropriate environment to flourish. In my experience the requisite bonding fails to occur in groups larger than about twelve, with eight to ten being the ideal size. One also needs sufficient curricular time: time for familiarization and confidence-building exercises, time for discussion of literary models and examples, and time for discussing students' work.

One also needs an agenda or syllabus. Here, once again, I must underline that I am talking about a creative writing strand in a literature degree, and not a verbal arts degree proper. In the Sheffield City Polytechnic

English degree, creative writing is a compulsory element (one of five) in the first two years and an option in the third. The syllabus is built on the premise of decreasing formality. In the first year students must complete ten set exercises. The first term, covering poetry, begins with exercises in strict meter and verse forms, ending in free and experimental verse; the second term, covering prose, includes exercises in the use of chronology, point of view and dialogue. Students submit a folder of their six best pieces. In the second year they are simply required to produce work in two different genres. In year three instead of the dissertation they may submit a folder of original work in a single genre with the proviso that the work is unified and that the student includes a short commentary describing their choice of subject-matter and saying why they have written about it in the way they have. About half of the students eligible to do so choose this option.

Creative writing, then, is not simply something that happens. It requires a structured syllabus and one has to be attentive to the nature of the seminar. The formal paradigm, stressing craft, invites analogies with other arts; as in painting, one begins with the basic techniques so that, once equipped, the student can push the frontiers of their expression in an informed way. The formal approach has the added benefit of relieving the stress on creativity: the focus for discussion falls on questions of technique rather than the specialness of the student's vision, imagination, sensitivity or mind. The discussion turns on whether the work works. There is a trade-off, for the approach can alienate students as too mechanical; but this, too, may become critical grist.

I now want to consolidate the argument that a creative writing course, structured in this way, with the above seminar model, is consonant with the drift of contemporary theory. I do not mean to say that a creative writing course spontaneously generates theory, but it does prompt the critical issues which engender theory. As an instance, take the case of writing creative prose. To begin with, a number of consequences flow from the protocol that students remain silent as their work is discussed. In effect the seminar reduplicates, in miniature, publishing. The benefit, from the writer's point of view, is the opportunity they receive of assessing how successfully they realized their intention, whether their intended effects came off. But from the point of view of the seminar the intention of the writer is irrelevant. The seminar members have only the work as they find it. Issues of evaluation naturally arise here, not just of whether a particular technique worked, but what it is that constitutes good writing. The situation is peculiarly rich. Say the class comes back to the writer, having formed their view. The writer may say they intended something quite different. The discussion may rest with the issue of technique – to express x, y would have been preferable – but it may also open up, theoretically. The difficult concept of 'voice', of the dialogic, may enter here. In a typical, teasingly apodictic passage from 'The Death of the Author,' Roland Barthes writes:

Writing is that neutral, composite, oblique space where our subject slips away, the negative where all identity is lost, starting with the very identity of the body writing . . . As soon as a fact is *narrated* no longer with a view of acting directly on reality but intransitively, that is to say, finally outside of any function other than that of the practice of the symbol itself, this disconnection occurs, the voice loses its origin, the author enters into his own death, writing begins.[1]

One of the most valuable things a creative writing seminar can accomplish is to engender this sense of where 'writing begins'. As Barthes indicates, writing begins with the author entering into his or her own 'death': they cease to write in their own voice, but in the voice of an other, one culturally produced, an other existing in advance of their mimicry, their impersonation, their assumption of a 'character'. One can put this very untheoretically indeed. It is what used to be called, is still called, having a 'good ear'. And one may observe, pragmatically, that some students, the 'natural' writers, enter into writing effortlessly: they have a knack, or talent. But this loss of one's own voice, the mimicry of an other, of turning one's own voice into a persona or character – of allowing narrative to perform this trick – is not, conceptually, self-evident.

The matter is further enriched by the overlay of genre. To give an instance, several years ago a mature woman student in one of my seminars produced what appeared to be a romantic story typical of the women's magazines it was, from her matronly appearance, easy to identify her with as her unreflecting reading matter. But the story had a kink in it. The group fought through its lazy reflex of projecting an intention on to the writer, getting to grips with the kink. What emerged was that the genre had it own sets of values, was itself a 'discourse', and that the story appeared to succeed in disrupting it was, satisfyingly, self-questioning. In Barthes's terms, what appeared to be 'readerly' was judged to be 'writerly', not soothing readerly preconceptions, but giving them a pleasurable jolt. The question of intention was nudged towards 'theory' (we ceased to ask after the author's 'message') while the criteria of evaluation substantially widened in scope. Genre also ceased to appear innocent. Practically it became evident that genres work as a series of conventions setting up expectations, which also raised the question of the desirability of breaking them in some measure. But theoretically it also became evident that genres are ideologically conditioned, obviously so in romance, but also conditioned elsewhere, if more subtly or less obviously. The link between genre and gender also emerged.

When I earlier asserted that there was an overlap between the drift of contemporary theory and the kinds of issues that emerge in a creative writing seminar, I had something like the above in mind. My purpose in sketching such a potential overlap was to nobble the hackneyed view (surely on its last legs) that teaching creative writing amounted to the encouragement of overflows of spontaneous emotion, while adding to the view that creative writing not only encouraged craft, but critical and finally theoretical thinking about craft. This leads to the further argument that a creative writing syllabus cannot only compete with practical criticism, but has certain, inbuilt advantages. For instance, it is possible to argue that the theoretical defamiliarization practical criticism is sometimes felt to be in need of inheres within a creative writing syllabus.

I now want to turn to the part of my argument that paradoxically states the reverse: that creative writing can also question theory and that, in terms of a unified curriculum, such questioning is a good thing.

In my experience, teaching of creative prose is kindly towards theory, but the teaching of poetry is comparatively resistant. The discipline of prose encourages a sense of the decentred subject, in Barthes's terms, the death of the personality as the writer strives after the creation of an intransitive space in which cultural and generic voices jostle and work against, or with, each other. But the gravity of poetry tends to the microscopically intentional. The discipline here is to think through rhythm and line length, through modulation and breakage, through the management of line, syntax and word choice. The relationship between poetic voice and colloquial voices, between idiom and culture, still holds, but tangentially so in comparison with prose. Writing poetry is, as it were, craft-intensive, even if that craft amounts to that loosening of the verbal and musical talents of the mind that think through the obliquities of language, its rhythmic, sonic and syntactic qualities. These 'raids on the inarticulate' often leave the raider inarticulate. The pleasure a class takes from its collective work often derives from the occasional mastery of language's marginal aspects, the expression of thoughts, feelings, ideas, tonalities, that cannot be said in other words. This pleasure naturally invites theoretical scrutiny, but the continual questioning of the right word, rhythm or line break drags discussion back to a view of the work as a series of decisions, of realized or unrealized intentions. This craft-intensiveness tends to recentre the subject.

I am not trying to make a hard and fast distinction between poetry and prose. On the contrary, although I believe the general point I am making does hold good, more or less, I can envisage circumstances in which the reverse might hold true. What I am trying to do is to rework in a modified way a point I made earlier when discussing the conflict between teaching creative writing from the point of view of a practising writer and teaching it from the vantage-point of a syllabus in a literature degree. I said then that the teaching of creative writing is both conducive and resistant to the kinds of critical issues contemporary theory has made us conversant with; and this doubleness, of teasing out and contradicting, is a peculiar aspect of the curricular fitness of teaching creative writing. Theory's easy abstractions, the tendency to turn theory into undifferentiated and undifferentiating sweeps, finds itself tested by the hard practicalities of writing.

In conclusion, I want to reiterate that creative writing is not an easy option, a break from theory's taxing disciplines. On the contrary it provides a natural focus for the critical issues that give theory its life. At the same time its practical element encourages close reading, an attentiveness to the peculiarities of form. A simple illustration of this occurs repeatedly every year among the admittedly more dedicated of my students who find, in the end, that there is no substitute for reading extensive quantities of poetry in order to begin to master the art of writing it. Before they can make their numbers speak they have to adjust their minds to speaking through numbers, sensing the inarticulate, not in the semantics or imagery, but in the rhythmic score; and this only occurs after serious immersion. *Mutatis mutandis*, the same can be said for prose. The students' practical critical sensitivities are thereby much improved. This seesaw between theory and craft, between critical and practical issues, in a peculiarly rich way satisfies the criteria I have lightly sketched in for the basis of an arts curriculum. Other, straight-forwardly pedagogic benefits also accrue. Involvement is more immediate than in straightforwardly critical studies. Texts are freed from the dead hand of 'literature', quickening again as 'writing' (so canonical texts can once more be seen as solutions to generic or expressive problems). The hierarchy of the seminar is broken down, inviting a democracy of judgement. In all these respects a structured creative writing course may complement the literary studies the student experiences elsewhere in the curriculum. I am not maintaining that existing close reading courses ought to be replaced immediately by creative writing ones. Such uniformity strikes me as undesir-able. My case, rather, is that the academic grounds for creative writing are every bit as strong as those supporting more traditional courses. Practical criticism has its peculiar virtues, but so does creative writing. An economically ordered curriculum will want to adjust the focus of its range of syllabuses to take advantage of each. As I have been arguing, theory and creative writing are complementary. A generic and cultural focus in literary studies, with a healthy segment of contemporary writing, would foster the tensed complementariness I have identified as a curricular good, while meeting the changing expectations of the emerging educational 'market'. One should not think of creative writing as a tasty extra with which to ice the curricular cake; the cake itself has to be rebaked. What emerges is both attractive and educationally compelling.

Note

1 Roland Barthes, 'The Death of the Author', *Image–Music–Text*, trans. Stephen Heath (Glasgow, Fontana, 1977) p. 142.

4

43%: A commentary on aims and assessments in the teaching of literary writing

— George Marsh —

> Bring out number, weight and measure in a year of dearth.
> (William Blake, *The Marriage of Heaven and Hell*)

Introduction

At the heart of tutoring literary writing is a relationship that is ideally like that between two writer friends, when one asks the other to advise on a manuscript before submitting it for publication. The 'tutor-friend' gives a deeply attentive reading, responds to the work so that the writer sees how it strikes one reader, identifies points where there is a lack of clarity and encourages the writer to feel confident about the areas of strength and build on them. The relationship depends on mutual trust and respect; it is rewarding and creative; it leaves the writer to make the final judgements; and the relationship is vulnerable. If, for example, the 'tutor-friend' is forced by bureaucratic demands into periodic attitudes of disrespect (such as affixing 43% to a poem) the relationship will suffer.

The teacher giving a low mark feels regretful and embarrassed, and fears that the mark, though given with integrity as a true judgement, will undermine the trust that was developing with the student. The student feels a shock. A mark of 43% does not say to the student: 'This piece is flawed and is not yet communicating as you want it to; together we can sort out the problems and, when you have redrafted, it will work!' Nor does it say, 'I think this piece is a dud and will never work. I suggest you do some development on that other idea you sketched out.' It says, 'You are 43%.' Scar tissue will grow over the hurt and the student will find ways to adjust (mixing with other low-mark students and disparaging the course, perhaps), but the delicate process of exchanging understandings until you have built mutual respect has been damaged and things that might have been brought to life may now not quicken in the student.

Sympathetic response is at the heart of the teaching and learning. Constraint, confused aims and inappropriate assessments can all obscure or distort the response. What follows is a commentary on some of the main categories of aims that writing courses adopt, the teaching methods implicit in those aims and the assessment issues that arise.

Please note: I am assuming for the purposes of this chapter that the reader is concerned with planning writing courses in higher education. The principles are very similar, however, in school-teaching, further education and continuing education.

Aim 1   'To train professional writers'

Commentary

If your students are vocational, planning will be relatively simple for you: the aim is clear and the criteria for success are clear; there is a sense of direction and a pay-off at the end. Only when the aims are more complex and uncertain does planning become problematic.

This aim will certainly not suit all students who want to study the subject, but has the virtue of implying a model of teaching: study should imitate the conditions of the professional activity. The tutor's role, for example, should be like that of a publisher's editor or agent, concerned with getting the script to work well for a particular audience, rather than with comparative judgement.

Implications for assessment

Professional writers are judged by publishers and then by readers. There is no such thing as 43% or 53% in the writer's world. The market will have quite different criteria from an institutionalized creative writing lecturer. Architects, designers, doctors, dancers, engineers and so on are assessed at present by the same form of standard degree assessment as everyone else in our higher-education culture: a classified degree system calculated from averaging or selecting percentage marks, with a fail mark at about 40%. But it is a bit of nonsense: designers get jobs by showing a portfolio; dancers by auditioning. Nobody cares about their tutors' assessments if they can do it. Engineers and doctors are moving towards change: you can get an engineering degree at 40+% by answering questions on a small proportion of the syllabus and getting all your calculations wrong. A 40% and-you-qualify system cannot assess competence for the professions and professional associations are beginning to make a fuss about it (Gibbs 1989).

There is no evidence that there is any correlation between degree classes and success in careers, except, in some cases, a negative correlation (Hoyt 1965, Taylor *et al.* 1965, Hudson, 1966a, Berg 1973; all quoted in Rowntree

1987: 19–20. See also Gibbs 1989: section 10). In higher education we are performing a useful social function selecting for the employment market, but we are deluding ourselves if we think we are doing it in the most useful way.

Norm-referenced assessments (like our present degrees, in which marks are manipulated so that a limited percentage of the candidates can get firsts, a limited percentage can fail, and the marks are distributed around the 'norm' on a standard distribution curve) are sure to give way soon to criterion-referenced ones (ones where a standard criterion is defined and everyone who meets that level is awarded the appropriate credit, regardless of how many other people reach it or fail to reach it). This will come about because of pressure from above and from below: from the professions, requiring defined standards of competence, and from the National Curriculum in schools, which has adopted criterion-referencing.

Criterion-referencing in creative writing assessment would mean that the institution would provide for each graduate a Profile of Achievement consisting of 'can-do' statements: 'This student can edit inessentials out of a draft and achieve clear statements in the active voice, with a good sense of rhetorically symmetrical phrasing and even of the strikingly epigrammatical.' A publisher would still judge by looking at the portfolio, but Profile can-do statements might be useful if the graduate applied, say, for a job which involved report writing or public relations. It would say much more than 'a two-two degree' says. But it would also be cumbersome, and there would no doubt be some absurdities entailed in writing the can-do statements about mysteriously beautiful artistic achievements.

Whatever form the final degree classification takes, the feedback to the student during the course could be of the kind that professional writers get: 'workshop' responses from peers; responses from a publications selection committee; publication; votes from readers of the departmental publications for their favourite item of the issue. There are two other principles for creative writing assessment which arise from analysing the nature of professional writing: the drafting principle and the sampling principle.

The drafting principle
Professional writing usually develops through several stages of drafting and incorporates responses to feedback. A piece of writing with major flaws rarely survives the critical scrutiny of helpful friends, editors and publishers: it is substantially revised in the light of their reactions. If educationists assess writing at an early stage in this process, give it a low mark because of avoidable flaws, and do not allow it to develop further but treat the grade as a final judgement no useful purpose is served. Unless the aim of the assessment is to 'catch out' the student by putting an unrealistic deadline on the writing and refusing to help the writer to succeed – a perverse view of an educator's responsibilities! – the method of evaluation should encourage high levels of achievement by *only grading when both parties are satisfied that the work has realized its full potential.*

The sampling principle

Anecdotal evidence from professional writers is that between one in four and one in ten of their projects comes to life and reaches its full glory. They throw away a lot; they publish flops; they succeed with one thing and get the next one rejected, and so on. Donald H. Graves (1983) publishes graphs showing the variability of quality in the writing of two children over two school years (pp. 261–2). The graphs zigzag up and down; there is no neat developmental progress curve. Graves and his researchers conclude that one in four or one in five pieces of writing done by children in school is what he terms 'hot'. He also finds that one of the children almost always followed a good piece with a 'downer', that there was significant seasonal variation and 'both children declined from April onward'. The clear conclusion to be drawn is that if you want your assessment system to tell you accurately what a writer is capable of when in good form you must not assess on one piece of work or one examination. You must sample from a selection of the best course work. Otherwise the grades you give will simply be misleading, however scrupulous you have been in your examination procedures – as misleading as judging Arsenal Football Club on one lost match or Gabriela Sabatini on a dropped service game.

Aim 2   'To illuminate criticism by learning experientially about the construction of a text'

Commentary

This aim has the virtue that it justifies the place of creative writing in a course which is centrally concerned with literary criticism. It suggests that the appropriate teaching strategy would be a series of technical exercises, probably arising out of the study of texts: writing the same passage from several points of view; translating direct speech into indirect speech and free indirect speech; writing metrical verses and writing in various stanza forms; working with imagery: the Imagist image, the Renaissance conceit, allegory and so on.

The writer's commentary on the writing would be as important as the writing itself, since the purpose is not to create works of art but to reflect on the ways texts are constructed. An unsuccessful piece of writing which led to insights about writing would be a success. One could end up in the absurd position where the central activity is not valued and rewarded, only the footnotes on it. Staff and students cannot maintain this view of writing. Staff get fed up with giving good marks to technically competent dead sonnets and tiresomely accurate heroic couplets, and students want to write expressively in forms shaped by the imperative of the theme and their contemporary idiom. Literature is much too lively to submit to the indignity of being used as a knife-grinder for critics.

Technique does not work anyway. People learn superficially when they focus on techniques, but successful 'deep' learners are those who are trying to make meaning of reality for themselves (Gibbs 1981: chapter 5). Literary writing without the primacy of meaning is a diet of cardboard sandwiches and will not nourish.

There is also *the principle of voluntarism* to respect: students who have en-rolled on a course in literary criticism and find themselves in a creative writing class might reasonably object (1) that you have not proved that writing improves criticism and (2) that a linguistics course, or a critical theory course, might be more useful.

Implications for assessment

One way of resolving the assessment problem is through hypocrisy: you assert the coherence of a creative element in a critical course (for CNAA, or whatever body asks you to be accountable) by saying that your aim is critical illumination, but teach and assess the writing course as though you were doing the writing for its own sake. This works up to a point, but still leaves you with a problem in justifying to the examinations board your desire to give a high grade for a living piece of free verse with an inadequate commentary and a lower one to a skilfully-made dead villanelle with a thorough critical commentary. Criterion-referenced assessment would not put you in this invidious position. You would simply state what was good about each piece of work; you would not need to rank them.

Strictly speaking, you need not assess the writing at all. It should stand or fall according to whether the criticism is judged to be better illuminated or not.

Aim 3   'To develop communication skills – a good command of language – valuable for many kinds of employment'

Commentary

This is by no means as pathetic as it looks. The Confederation of British Industry (CBI), the government, the careers services, the CNAA, the Universities Funding Council and business people everywhere constantly repeat that it is one of the main things employers seek in a graduate. It is an extremely valuable skill in the market-place, one well worth boasting about. The argument that you can train students effectively (and you can) will impress the hard-nosed nominees from commerce on governing bodies and vetting committees – or, rather, it will impress academic managers who take it upon themselves to speak for what the commercial people want and are much more hard-nosed than the business people themselves are.

There are three problems with stating the aim this way. It is not sufficient in itself. It is not the foremost thing in the minds of staff and students when they are doing it – for reasons outlined above under Aim 2, literary writing dies if it is thought of as *just* useful, even though it is useful. And it appears to lead towards employment-related forms of writing such as the report or the public relations handout, though there are perfectly good reasons for resisting this drift.

Implications for assessment

There are not, however, good reasons for resisting the 'useful' criterion in assessment. You can argue that you are aiming at efficient communication skills by taking a roundabout route through literary writing (instead of the more functional forms of writing used in business) because you believe that literary writing is more motivating, teaches the desired skills at the most demanding level and because no one resents spending lavish amounts of time and effort on the necessary redrafting of something he or she sees as personally meaningful. But you cannot argue that the assessment should not test the declared aim. You should be rewarding efficiency and skills, not making artistic judgements. In practice the problem is most unlikely to lead to any conflict, but it is an indication that there is an inconsistency here and this aim cannot be free-standing.

Aim 4 'That learners do literary writing . . . because it is intrinsically worthwhile'

Commentary

This is the real aim of those of us who are teaching it because we love it. Whereas this aim is appropriate in a degree called 'Literary Writing' on which only students who selected it are enrolled, it is not enough to justify literary writing as a contributory element in a course students have chosen for another reason. There are thousands of things which some people think are intrinsically worthwhile, from first aid and jogging to prayer, but they cannot all be crammed into every course. Peter Abbs, amongst others (Abbs 1989a), has made out a case for the arts subjects being *more* intrinsically worthwhile than other activities, but at college age I feel the principle should be voluntarism.

Implications for assessment

This aim leaves you free to make judgements in the way in which you want: on the basis of a sense of the wholeness of the piece of writing and its qualities as what-it-is, not what-skills-it-displays.

Experience in the assessment of creative work (in dance, drama, art and music) suggests that grading can be done successfully (whether it should is another issue). Moderators 'blind marking' have enough consistency of judgement to show that there is a high level of reliability, but in a small proportion of cases there are very pronounced variations between markers. It is now standard practice in the arts to have two or three assessors involved in material judgements on creative work. As long as we double-mark, and moderate where there is a difference between the two markers, we can be relatively confident about applying consistent standards in the assessment of literary writing.

If we claim we are dealing with works of art, however, we have to be careful about what form of assessment will be acceptable. Some works of art and some artists are no doubt robust enough to take a hailstorm of surly percentage grades; the sensitive plant and the tentative plant will be battered to the ground. It cannot be the best environment in which to grow thriving poems and plays. They like standing ovations and tears in the eye. It raises the question: who is the assessment for?

If it is for *the artist* then it must serve two functions: to encourage development, and to give realistic feedback. Feedback is much better, it seems to me, coming from *many* people than from one, and from peers or interested readers rather than someone in authority, a lecturer. The writer will listen more attentively to the reader he or she respects most, of course, and if that person is the lecturer then so much the better. But the comment will be valued because the commentator is valued, not because the institutional hierarchy gives that commentator grading privileges. Feedback is also far more help if it is verbal and precise than if it is a mysterious 53%. Does that mean brilliant in flashes but flawed in structure and phrasing, or terribly dull but quite well structured and phrased?

If the assessment is for *the outside world of employment* (degrees are the education system's way of sorting recruits for society) then it must (for the present, at least) fall into the conventional pattern of classification. Ideally we would design assessments which encouraged students and developed their writing during the three years of the course ('formative' assessments, in the jargon) and a classified end assessment which judged the final achieved quality ('summative' assessment, in the jargon). But with everything hanging on the summative assessment, there is a great danger of the tail wagging the dog: students who are going to be assessed in percentages at the end will want to be prepared properly, and to have practice in meeting the criteria of judgement used in grading the degree. There is really no excuse for not making the course a preparation for the degree. The inconsistency of saying, 'We will assess one way throughout the degree to encourage your learning, but another way when it matters most' will put terrible pressure on the rationale for the teaching. We should really assess in a way that is consistent with our declared aims and our teaching methods.

If the assessment is for *institutional monitoring and record keeping* it does not need to be represented by a grade number. Large bureaucracies find numbers easier to collect and sort (which is probably why we *are* grading), but personal tutors in human-sized institutions find verbal comments on work more informative for the purposes of reviewing a student's progress than grades.

The present system purports to be grading for the world of employment – a very dubious claim, given the evidence of how employers react. In fact the only group that benefits from the grading system is the staff. It gives staff status; they are those who practise judgement and assign a numerical value to the quality of mind of every professional recruit in the country. They are proud of their powers of discrimination. They fondly imagine that they are objectively discerning the true nature of things in a world of hierarchies. They mistake the signifier for the signified, forgetting that a semiotic system can be internally coherent and meaningful, like any one of several self-contained but mutually contradictory mathematical systems, but bear no relation to 'reality'. The sophisticated ones will acknowledge that objectivity is a slippery concept and that they are relativists and so on and so forth, but they still behave *as if* they were judging objective truths – or why would they persist? Even if you know it is nonsense, it is still gratifying to have so much social importance for doing it.

Aim 5   'To teach literary writing . . .'

Commentary

Only a slight change of wording here indicates an important shift of emphasis. To 'teach' writing implies that there is a body of knowledge called writing which we can teach. It also implies that the structure of the course will naturally follow the epistemology of 'writing'. If we can persuade ourselves that there is such an unproblematic structure of given knowledge and we fix our attention upon the subject rather than the student, then problems of planning and assessment disappear. The planning becomes a matter of organizing the body of knowledge coherently and the assessment becomes a matter of seeing whether they know it or not. There are still many people in literary criticism and linguistics departments who conceive of their teaching in these terms, but it is almost impossible to imagine any of the creative arts subjects being successfully incorporated into this paradigm. We will pass quickly on.

Aim 6   'To develop the mind of the student', or 'to develop imagination and creativity'

Commentary

All education seeks to develop the mind, but it used to be argued from Roman times to the end of the nineteenth century that the best way of doing it was through the study of rhetoric: a gentleman at university learned to write formally disciplined verses in Greek and Latin, to study philosophical argument, to use language with precision and to do translations into effective English. This wonderful early version of a Verbal Arts degree eventually got the blame, however, for the loss of empire and the decline of Britain as an industrial power. It has never recovered. The story is that it produced a lot of Sir Humphreys (of *Yes, Prime Minister*) who were specious, snobbish clever-dicks disdaining technology. Competitor nations got on with training scientists and engineers while our elite class frittered away its education making exquisitely tasteful and eloquent excuses.

It is a brave course planner who writes down the aim, 'to develop imagination'. Those on the vetting committee are sure to pounce on the word and demand to know what it really means and what you know about the conditions in which it develops. There is a strong defence, and Peter Abbs is at the moment engaged in the heroic enterprise of articulating it in more than ten volumes (Abbs 1987, Abbs 1989a and b etc.). We all owe him a debt of gratitude. He is precise and consistent in his use of the terminology, but many crimes have been committed in the past in the name of the 'imagination' and sceptics have a right to ask hard questions.

The Cox Report and the National Curriculum for English which grew out of it have also wisely avoided the terms. We believe that literary writing is concerned with imaginative qualities – of course we do – but we are on safer ground if we say we are aiming at good writing, and define what that is, than if we try to isolate supposed features of 'the imagination' divorced from the context of the piece of writing.

The terms 'imagination' and 'creativity' can be politically useful. They are among the 'personal transferable skills' which the employers' associations seek in graduates, along with communications skills. Whether there is yet any real acceptance that 'creativity' is 'transferable' is doubtful, however. What will the managing director of a light engineering firm say when a candidate for a job claims that he or she can come up with creative solutions to design and manufacturing problems, 'because I can write a poem'? And how many Engineering Faculties have recently invited you to offer a poetry-writing course on their degrees to develop the imaginative, problem-solving side of their students?

Implications for assessment

'Quality of mind', 'imagination' and 'creativity' are self-justifying phrases allowing you to say that whatever you choose to reward in your assessment demonstrates these characteristics. If you can get away with stating your aims in these terms you will not have any restrictions on your assessment criteria. Students will not find any helpful guidance in such criteria, however. The ones with flair and confidence will not worry, but the more uncertain ones will despair when told that all they need to do to improve their grades is to be 'more imaginative'.

Aim 7 'To prepare school-teachers for teaching creative writing'

Commentary

The Kingman Report on the *Teaching of English Language* (DES 1988: 70) recommended that 'before the end of the century a prerequisite for entry to the teaching profession as an English specialist should normally be a first degree in English which incorporates a study of both contemporary and historical linguistic form and use'. The Cox Report (DES 1989), which superseded Kingman, did not specify what features must appear in English degrees acceptable as qualifications for intending teachers but established both knowledge about language and creative writing centrally in the schools' National Curriculum and said that teachers of writing should be writers themselves. The implication is clear. Creative writing should appear not just in teacher training courses but in first degrees which claim to give competence in 'English'.

This aim justifies dealing with literary writing for what it is, not for its supposed incidental benefits, and encouraging learning about each of the major genres from experience of using them. It has further implications too: that the rationale for teaching is made explicit; that the teacher should 'model' (1) what a writer does (such as keep a journal, agonize over choice of subject and redraft) and (2) what a teacher of writing does; and that the principles of assessment should be exposed to view and open to debate so that future teachers have a perspective on the whole process.

The Cox Report urges schools to do 'aesthetic and imaginative writing' and makes many references to the value of doing stories and poems in particular. It encourages 'play with language, for example by making up jingles, poems, word games, riddles . . .' (17.39) and states that 'the best writing is vigorous, committed, honest and interesting' (17.31), while excusing itself from mapping these qualities on to formal statements of attainment for assessment. It repeatedly emphasizes the importance of re-drafting – the one really radical departure in its treatment of the traditional English curriculum. But it does not state any aims for literary writing (it is much better on the aims of literary reading). It evades the 'imagination' issue and also evades the 'quality' issue.

Implications for assessment

The 'Attainment Targets' for writing at the National Curriculum's progressively higher levels are defined in terms of the complexity of the task and the mastery of processes, not in terms of quality. At Level 2, for instance, young children should be able to 'write stories showing an understanding of the rudiments of story structure by establishing an opening, characters, and one or more events' and at Level 4 they should be able to 'write stories which have an opening, a setting, characters, a series of events and a resolution'. It is easy to lose patience with the explicitness and avoidance of qualitative judgements of these criteria (why not say a 'better' story!) but there is a most important principle at work; one which will revolutionize our cultural attitudes to competition and achievement.

Making criteria absolutely explicit, even if it involves stating what to us seems obvious, in long-winded clumsy language, is a way of enfranchizing those who have always found the aims and methods of judgement of the education system mysterious. Elites perpetuate themselves by leaving matters such as how you are selected for advancement to nods and winks and tacit understandings. Now the things you have to learn are there, exposed to view, uncluttered by the terminology we have always wrapped them in in the past ('sensitive', 'fine', 'brilliant') and for many who want to know what they must do to make progress it will be an important step towards liberation. The removal of the qualitative terms also signals that the assessment system is geared to enabling people to be rewarded for what they can demonstrate they can do, not for being better or worse than others, half way up or down the humiliation scale. The shift from an emphasis on 'can't-do' marking systems to 'can-do' ones is as important to the cause of educational rights as the shift from a presumption of guilt to a presumption of innocence was to legal rights. 'For a few to emerge as outstandingly successful the majority must fail – to varying degrees' (Rowntree 1987). This is not the place to go into a detailed account of the psychological and social consequences of manufacturing failure on such a massive scale as we do. Suffice it to say that it is not the way to get the best out of people and make them feel good. Dr Samuel Johnson put it succinctly: 'By exciting emulation and comparisons of superiority, you lay the foundation of lasting mischief; you make brothers and sisters hate each other' (quoted in Rowntree 1987).

Criterion-referenced assessment is rather cumbersome, and may appear circumlocutory (because it avoids saying 'bad'), but we shall all get better at writing it (and interpreting it when reading it!) as we gain experience. Take the following example, concerning a sixteen-year-old school leaver, from one of the schools that pioneered profiling in the early 1980s:

> While writing does not come easily to Chris, he has made significant progress. He is very pleased to have made his script cursive, a reasonable size, fairly regular, and legible. His spelling is sufficiently accurate to cause no impediment to understanding, and punctuation of sentences supports his sensible presentation of meaning. He can now tackle writing tasks with every expectation of conveying his points successfully.
>
> (Blanchard 1986)

This gives a clear picture of the level of literacy of one of those who, under any other educational regime, would have simply been called a failure. It does not fudge the issue. It gives more useful information than a failure grade. It leaves the student's dignity intact. And it is psychologically healthier for the assessing members of staff to be involved in respecting those whom they serve than in disparaging them.

For the time being, while we are still stuck with classified norm-referenced degrees in higher education, our principle should be to do what we can to mitigate the effects of graded assessment. We should avoid over-assessing (constant and demanding continuous assessments *plus* a full diet of examinations are still used in my local polytechnic literature department). We should watch out for the signs of assessment anxiety syndrome. The classic case of the syndrome's lifelong effects is Colonel Cathcart in *Catch-22* (Heller 1962):

Colonel Cathcart was conceited because he was a full colonel with a combat command at the age of only thirty-six; and Colonel Cathcart was dejected because although he was already thirty-six he was still only a full colonel. Colonel Cathcart was impervious to absolutes. He could measure his own progress only in relation to others . . . The fact that there were thousands of men his own age and older who had not even attained the rank of major enlivened him with foppish delight in his own remarkable worth; on the other hand, the fact that there were men of his own age and younger who were already generals contaminated him with an agonising sense of failure and made him gnaw at his fingernails with an unappeasable anxiety . . .

Conclusions concerning assessment

Pass/fail assessment is a branch of dualism, a philosophical dead-end. It is as modern and liberating as a belief in condemning to hell-fire for all eternity everyone who feels randy.

There should certainly be minimum competency requirements for airline pilots, doctors and university vice-chancellors (these last, for example, should have read a book on assessment at some time, and should be able to demonstrate some knowledge of learning theory) but there is no need to institutionalize *failure* as a cultural norm for the majority of the population. The fact that we know it is possible to do it, with infinitely fine discrimination, is not sufficient justification. Schoolteachers and the National Curriculum for schools have given us an inspiring lead by reforming their assessment practices. Much of higher education is a long way behind, and blissfully unaware of it.

The participation rate in higher education is set to more than double, if the government can achieve its aims. There are politicians and senior academics assuring us that 'standards', represented by degree grading conventions, will not decline. Such assertions imply that it is possible, within the normal distribution curve, to infinitely expand the third class and lower second class categories to cater for increased numbers of academically weak students. The mistake is to view everything with the talented student in mind and hope that the long 'tail' in the class can still just be squeezed through. But if we look instead at what is best for the hordes who will perform, if we retain our present 'standards', at 40%–50%, the inappropriateness is clear.

The giving of high grades can be stimulating. But what is the effect of giving a string of grades like 43%? Bare pass marks are at present given to inadequate work to avoid the embarrassment of failing students. They signal to the students that they are not considered bright and are doing very badly, but *passing*. Imagine the confusion that must create in the student's mind! It is a painful situation for the educator (never mind the learner!)

to be involved in an exchange that amounts to saying, 'There is an awful lot wrong with you. The assessment system does not give me a chance to tutor you through several drafts. This miserable first attempt you have submitted is lacking in confidence – and no wonder – and misconceives the whole task. I am sure you *could* put it right and meet the basic criteria for completing the task adequately, but the relentless list of deadlines for essays rolls on and there is no time to do anything now but to arrest the development of this piece of writing before it has even woken up to what it is, fix a humiliating grade on you and remind you that your next assignment has to be in on Friday because I must get the final grades to the examiner by Whitsun week. Next please.'

One advantage we have, in the discipline of literary writing, is a body of staff who are all strongly committed to the drafting principle. The assessment system we inherit from the critical disciplines is inappropriate to drafting: it sets arbitrary deadlines and halts the development of drafts at those points. If we are true to the nature of our discipline, we will surely reform cut-off date assessments that force us into the absurd position of giving very poor 'pass' grades to work which should be recast entirely and used as a learning experience. I cannot imagine anything more appalling than maintaining present 'standards' through an enormous expansion in the higher education system and repeating the damaging and pointless exercise of fixing 43% on the work of another million young hopefuls.

People learn by being stretched and solving problems. Grades that arrest the process do not help. If the criteria were clear when the work was set and the writing does not meet the criteria, what is gained by giving a grudging low pass? The work should be returned and the student given the opportunity to succeed, to get to the stage where there is a lot to praise and admire.

Summary of conclusion

1. Assessment throughout the course should be 'formative'; that is, the audience for it is the student and it is directed to developing the student's learning. This assessment is essentially a form of dialogue and the student has a voice in it: a right to contribute.
2. The drafting principle should be enshrined in the assessment system: a student has the right to develop the work as far as he or she can before being judged.
3. 'Summative' assessment at the end of the course, for other audiences, should be consistent with formative assessment or it will distort the curriculum. A Profile of Achievement stating what the student can do is consistent with constructive formative assessments.
4. Summative assessment should give a picture of what the student can do, not a mysteriously authoritative number that represents how far short of the Platonic ideal the student falls (and will always fall, it implies).

5   Higher education should follow the excellent example of the schools' National Curriculum and assess using criterion-referencing and a series of set 'levels'. A student is given a Level 8 credit when Level 8 has been reached, a Level 10 when Level 10 has been reached, not a date on which he or she will be measured against faster students and found wanting.

6   Assessment of literary writing should respect the sampling principle. Not all work is of the same quality and work done on demand in a limited time in an examination is usually of much lower quality than the best work done under ideal conditions. A student has the right to be judged on what he or she can do and the basis for assessment should therefore be a selection of best course work.

7   Courses should have flexible timescales. The arbitrary deadline for examining settled on by our institutional bureaucracy makes us fail, or give dispiriting grades to, people who are making progress but are only two-thirds of the way along the path. It cuts off development.

8   Staff are there to serve students and help students to grow in competence and confidence. Hurting them with grade judgements has no place in this process. If students ask for a realistic assessment of how they stand in relation to others they should be told, but if they are receiving detailed verbal feedback (1) and credits for reaching set levels (5) there is unlikely to be much demand for grading.

References

Abbs, Peter (ed.)(1987). *Living Powers*. Lewes, Falmer Press.
Abbs, Peter (1989a). *A is for Aesthetic*. Lewes, Falmer Press.
Abbs, Peter (ed.) (1989b). *The Symbolic Order*. Lewes, Falmer Press, and the volumes of The Falmer Press Library on Aesthetic Education.
Blanchard, John (1986). *Out in the Open: A Secondary English Curriculum*. Cambridge, Cambridge University Press.
DES (1988). *Report of the Committee of Inquiry into the Teaching of English Language* (The Kingman Report). London, HMSO.
DES (1989). *English for Ages 5 to 16* (The Cox Report). London, Department of Education and Science and the Welsh Office.
Gibbs, Graham (1981). *Teaching Students to Learn*. Milton Keynes, Open University Press.
Gibbs, Graham (1989). 'Module 3, Assessment', from *Certificate in Teaching by Open Learning*, Oxford Centre for Staff Development, Oxford Polytechnic.
Graves, Donald H. (1983). *Writing: Teachers and Children at Work*. Oxford, Heinemann Educational.
Heller, Joseph (1962). *Catch-22*. London, Jonathan Cape.
Rowntree, Derek (1987). *Assessing Students: How Shall we Know Them?* 2nd edn. London, Kogan Page.

5

The American experience

Janet Burroway

I

At the Emerson Grammar School in Phoenix, Arizona, I told my seventh grade literature teacher that I wrote poems. Mr Allsworth (his first name lost to memory, though I can still see his drift and bobble of white hair) looked at my efforts and pronounced my instinct for rhyme and rhythm good, but found me ignorant of prosody. For several months of that warm winter of 1948 I stayed after school on Thursday afternoons while Mr Allsworth taught me the poetic feet. I had always sought to be 'teacher's pet', and had always understood that this status was compensation for some deep lack. But these afternoons did not seem to be related to ordinary lessons; they marked me out as special in some new way. I remember those anapaestic Arabs who folded up their tents and stole away. I felt that the names of dactyl and dimeter, caesura, alexandrine, were arcane knowledge, akin to spells and incantations. It did not occur to me that I might be learning a branch of the teaching trade.

But at about the time Mr Allsworth sat drumming iambs on the wood top desk in the empty classroom, 'creative writing' was being invented as a profession in a number of innovative American universities. A scattering of such courses had been taught as early as the turn of the century, in particular by George Pierce Baker at Harvard, whose classes in practical playwrighting had influenced a whole generation of American dramatists, and who had been lured to Yale in 1933 by the promise of a serious university-based School of Drama. The stage, however, was a complex worldly medium, and might not be tainted by teaching, whereas college courses in fiction and poetry were still not quite respectable. These so-called creative writing courses had a reputation for hack work and commerciality, they were thought to be 'trade' in the manner of a woodworking or motor mechanics course; their teachers were accused of serving the low standards of *The Saturday Evening Post* or *The Ladies' Home Journal* and in many instances no doubt this was the case. Writing as Literature, it was supposed, 'could not be taught' and was not properly pursued in a university.

It was Paul Engle at the University of Iowa who challenged both that cliché and another: 'Them as can, do, them as can't, teach.' The founding of the Iowa Writers' Workshop under Engle's direction in 1944 is generally seen as the turning-point in the study of fiction and poetry writing in America. Engle's simple idea was that practising writers should teach writing, and that the university should offer writers a home in which to do so. His ambitious goal was to legitimize the making of literature into the academic stream.

The early results of Engle's experiment were so encouraging that, little by little, and in far more partial and timid ways, the idea spread – a course in fiction here, a resident poet there, a reading series, a novelist on the staff. By the time I came to Barnard College in New York in the mid-1950s, two habits – not yet institutions – had been adopted in the city: the public reading of poetry and fiction, and the offering of courses in those genres. At the Poetry Center of the Young Men's Hebrew Association I made coffee and onion dip for the Young Writers' Reading Series (Truman Capote, Walker Percy, Donald Hall) and took courses from Louise Bogan, Rolfe Humphries, W.H. Auden. At Barnard I studied fiction writing with Hortense Calisher, poetry with Leonie Adams, composition with George Plimpton and playwrighting with Howard Teichmann.

In the 1960s, which I spent mostly in England, I often found myself defending the notion of creative writing as a university subject and also often critiquing a Sussex student's fiction or poetry – occasionally at the same time. In America in that period creative writing 'programs' – that is, writing as a recognizable course of study, a major, or field, or 'concentration' – appeared in a growing number of private and state universities, principally in the mid-west and the south. The teaching of writing, for good or ill, became a sinecure for increasing numbers of American writers – and whether for good or ill became the subject of much controversy, a subject in its own right for academic articles, reviews and bombast.

In 1967, R.V. Cassill of Brown University gathered a dozen interested colleges into the Associated Writing Programs of America. AWP became important as a means of contact between writers separated by several hundred or thousand miles, sometimes isolated in small communities, as the new profession continued to expand rapidly throughout the 1970s. AWP doubled and quadrupled its membership, put out a newsletter, a job list, sponsored an anthology to make the best of the writing from its programs available nationwide, then a series of contests for book-length manuscripts in the various genres, a catalogue of programs, and an annual meeting at which teaching writers could exchange ideas on literature, writing and the teaching of literature and writing.

By the time I returned from Sussex to teach in Florida State University in 1971, creative writing was the hottest subject in the English department – 'the boom trade of the English bizz' as one not entirely approving colleague put it. (At Florida State, the linguistics program had died off for lack of student interest and university support, but the department's commitment to a writing program carried through the energy crisis and massive cut-backs.) Student demand was high. Programs typically included fiction, poetry and drama; in some institutions the writing of non-fiction was also taught under the rubric of creative writing and in some screen and television were taught along with playwrighting for the stage. AWP and many universities argued for the Master of Fine Arts in Writing as a terminal degree; others kept the literature requirements and offered an MA and/or a PhD with a creative thesis/dissertation. Some programs were 'studio-oriented', like Iowa's, with rigorous writing demands and literature courses offered largely as electives; others were more conventional in their literary offerings but gave ample time and credit for imaginative writing. By the late 1980s AWP had 198 institutional members and 328 programs listed in its catalogue, and by that time, also, creative writing teachers constituted the old guard.

The self-styled Martians of the 1960s have now taken up the burdens of the mainstream academic: advising, curriculum and administration; and the controversy over creative writing has been taken up between the writers and the theorists. At my own university writing students, at both the graduate and the undergraduate level, make up nearly half the population in the English department. There are by now half a dozen on the staff better qualified than I to teach prosody, and I stick to fiction and drama. But I partly know that this critical examination of scenes and stories, this insisting on specifics and circling of clichés, is a decent endeavour, because somewhere in it Mr Allsworth sits (first name forgotten), drumming iambs on my formica.

II

The student at my desk-side chair has pale hair she drags between thumb and finger. One shin is wrapped around the other under a stonewashed skirt. 'I'm ashamed to show it to you,' she says. 'I can't get it right.' Her shame blotches her neck. 'I try and try; it just *won't . . .*' This young woman is talented. She has a quirky command of imagery, wry dialogue at once sexy and sinister; her apathetic characters do credibly violent things. She begins to cry.

The young man has black hair slicked back. He frisbees the manuscript on to my desk. 'This is an extra,' he says for the third time this week. 'Take a look. I think you'll get a kick out of it.' His ankles articulate like hinges under the rungs of the chair. His eyes zap my computer screen. His stuff is bratpack slick and turbo-paced and thin. He already self-publishes a magazine on the Macintosh his Dad sent up from Miami. An A in the course matters to him more than sex or money.

This one has vague eyes – grass? madness? mere preoccupation? – and his hair is a congregation of cowlicks. 'What I thought; the *doorbell* . . . but I don't know. He comes around to see them, right, it's not clear why. Does he stay, that's the thing. You think?' The tale whereof he speaks is a wildly brilliant mess. Its so-called plot wanders and flails, its surreal personages leer and galumph in a setting sired by Kafka out of Djuna Barnes; the language flares like an accident in a fireworks factory. 'I know, like you said, *form*, but . . .'

These students will pass into the insurance industry, academia, counselling, husbandry, wifery, public relations, drug-running, state government. Or not. They will continue to write. Or not. For each one of them (and the other dozen in the workshop) I could years hence construct a thumbnail sketch with the message that he/she was recognizably a writer in the making. I know enough not to take any bets on which one I will be asked to write it for. At the end of two or three years in the Writing Program, some who arrived with talent will not have moved on, while some who showed nothing but dedication and cliché will have become writers. Some will have acquired the dedication. Some will make an evolutionary leap. If my students have taught me one thing in 20 years of teaching writing, it is that though I can assess their achievement I cannot predict it. If they have taught me two things, the humbling second is that the desire to write in all its modes – ferocity, arrogance, self-doubt, determination, dull despair – bears no relation whatever to ability. We share it all alike.

As a student in the 1950s I was, unconsciously, committed to the American notion of a 'star system', which is only a vulgar manifestation of a 'canon'. I was greedy for the creative writing courses that were just beginning to be respectable because I thought they could show me how to be a 'great' writer. When I went on to study in England I was doubly struck with the unpretentious workaday attitudes of writers and actors, and with the respect that the professional worlds in those two spheres accorded beginners. (England has learned a poor lesson from us in this respect, and it now seems to me that there's both a star system and a closed shop.)

But later, on the other side of the podium, I still saw my job as imparting some of the skills of writing to students generally, while I waited for the star student whom I would then help to become a professional and who would provide the *raison d'être* of my teaching. Now I see it otherwise.

Like most of my colleagues in the American Writing Program boom of the 1970s and 1980s, I have felt a nagging ambivalence about the teaching of creative writing. Are we giving false hopes to untalented young writers and spawning dozens of little magazines produced by people who cannot otherwise get published for the entertainment of their amateurish friends? Or are we the monks of the new Dark Ages, keeping the language alive in our workshop cloisters? Is the truth somewhere in the middle, or at both extremes?

Then at some point I began to hold the 'little' magazines in high regard. As telecommunications swallow the custom of writing letters, the least professional of the literary journals are a kind of correspondence; and as the corporate giants swallow the trade publishers, the best provide an alternative place for good writers to get published.

In the classroom, I saw that I could interest writers in reading, and would need to. Literacy is receding even as we realize that our ideas of literature are provincial. Both literature and creative writing will now have to be taught in universities for the same reason that philosophy is taught; because they are not part of the everyday experience of most people. I observed as a curious paradox, as if it were unconnected, that students with shaky values and small evidence of literary taste could nevertheless out of their massive television experience turn a joke, tag a character, shape a plot, produce a recognition scene, foreshadow, plant, reveal, betray a truth through a stage lie.

It now seems to me not a curiosity and not merely inexplicable, but a mystery, that students who have not read nevertheless arrive at university wanting, often passionately, to write. They have some kind of connection with the language that is not satisfied by the passive relationship they have had to it through TV. Television is ineluctably seductive. It usurps entire the escape function of literature which was always its first lure, and it does so promising that the escape costs no effort. But by the time these people are 18 or 20 they have been cheated the way people are cheated by drugs: the effortlessness leaves emptiness. You do not own it if you have not put any energy into it. And so they come wanting to write. Yes, they want to 'express themselves' – there is a therapeutic aspect in all writing – but they also perceive, perhaps dimly, that language has to do with being human, and that they need it at the deepest level, for identity.

In a 1985 survey done for the National Endowment for the Arts, it was shown that 25% of the adults in America believe they write fiction or poetry. *25% of the adults in America believe they write fiction or poetry.* This cannot be true. But it argues for more than widespread self-deception. People used to put a lot of effort into writing letters that had an audience of one. Few now think there is much point in writing letters. But in spite of the grim garbagey things that are being done with and to the language by all the wielders of pomp, power and finance, people still want to connect through the written word.

The backlash against creative writing is in full flood. Like any backlash it has the substance of the original prejudice in a slightly more sophisticated form. Whereas the fiction courses of the 1940s were supposed to produce formula adventure for pulp magazines, those of the 1980s are charged with producing formula pap for literary magazines.

To Donald Morton and Mas'ud Zavarzadeh, the creative writing workshop fosters only realism, of which minimalism is a subset; for Tom Wolfe the workshop prevents realism, of which minimalism is the antithesis. Joseph Epstein deplores an atmosphere that dictates against genius; the chorus of post-modernists hoots down the notion of genius as hegemony, but agrees that writing stories is too *soft*.

My students do not read this controversy much – they tend to read Gustave Flaubert, Eudora Welty and Margaret Atwood – and when they do it does not produce any shiver of recognition. I do not recognise it either. It is true that, on the road to competence, students (and perhaps magazines, decades, media) often pass through a period in which they try each other's strengths and ape each other's successes. It is a kind of learning. Some never get beyond it. But it would be a gross misreading of young writers to suppose that they cannot recognize, or do not reward, genuine originality.

One of the things the condemnations of writing programs have in common is a punitive attitude towards those who want to write without having what the critics consider sufficient talent. This is the only-geniuses-need-apply view of fiction and poetry. It is certainly true that many students' desire to write is tainted by false reverence toward writers and artists, a fuzzy notion of genius, and a bedazzlement by celebrity. The students thus fooled attach themselves to writing as to a talisman of magical ascent. But the set of false assumptions they ascribe to is not different from that of the critics who want to scold them for attempting to write. It is the same set. Both sides use the name of Writer for purposes of name-dropping; they mean to ennoble themselves by knowing it.

Whatever else it argues, the case against creative writing assumes that competence will prevent rather than promote excellence. This seems to me preposterous as a general idea, and it is not what I see happening in the classroom, which is that competence, excellence and originality grow together. In Bali everybody's a dancer. It is very good for Bali, and for dance.

Certainly the imaginative activity in the ivory tower has an effect on the world that is commonly referred to as real. The function of the New York and Boston publishers has changed. As the great trade houses knuckle under to their accountants, the university and 'little' presses become prestigious places to publish, and the former continue to make writers rich and famous. This they have always done; but they also used to choose who to do it to. Now the nationwide complex of writing programs, conferences and literary magazines gently floats their best towards the east. Clever New York agents and editors show up at the headwaters and backwaters in Iowa City, Salt Lake, Austin and Tallahassee.

Basically this pleases and amuses me, though I tell my students that literary success is also a great crap shoot; and in the classroom we do not spend a lot of time talking about it. I used to say quite blithely, 'Of course, you can't teach *talent*', but now I am less sure what talent is, and about its relation to models and criticism and encouragement. Good writing comes from an ability to connect the interior richness of which all of us are possessed – *all* – with the structure of the language. Creative writing is taught when a teacher helps a student make that connection through verse or story or the stage. This happens only sometimes, but there seems to be no limit to the ways that it can happen.

Sports and literature are the two great surrogates for war, exercising without disaster the impulses toward struggle, competition, the triumph of survival. Business is too tainted with power on the one hand and the possibility of subsistence failure on the other to operate as a metaphor; the arts outside literature are not to the same degree dependent on the concepts of struggle and endurance. We need surrogates for war, and it is good to have a choice. Some people are good at sports and some are good at stories. Writing ought, in my view, to hold a position in our society more or less like playing tennis. A passable amateur tennis player may exercise her skill often, even obsessively, can involve some few others as partners and spectators, can struggle to improve and feel exhilarated by the struggle. It is impressive if she turns professional, but no one despises her for devoting a portion of most days to the game, even if no one will ever pay money to watch her play. Nobody says that, because tennis requires innate talent, the weekend buff is an embarrassment.

By the same token, the amateur – that is, the lover of the game – does not suppose that, because he can catch felt on catgut three returns out of five, he is just a lucky break away from Wimbledon. He does it for the doing. Because, although it is hard to get revved up for it, once you start the momentum carries you; because you get better when you work at it; because the effort makes you sweat and it feels good to have done it. I think we ought to think of writing more like that.

My own expectations as a teacher of writing are quite modest. I only want my students, when they leave me, to write with more accuracy, more eloquence, more originality, and a better sense of the relationship between their language and their truth, than the President of the United States. In the 20 years I have been teaching this has not been too much to ask.

6

Creative writing and assessment: A case study

John Singleton

Introduction

From its tentative beginnings in the late 1970s as a minor option within English, Writing at Crewe and Alsager has grown to its present position as a major independent subject, with 200 students distributed across four separate degree programmes. At present Writing constitutes a minimum of one-third of students' study and can, in the final year, make up two-thirds of their academic work. The subject now covers every mode of composition – verse and prose fiction, film/TV/stage/radio scripting, feature articles and interviews, travel and autobiographic writing, reportage and reviewing. To cope with an increasing range of work and the recent expansion in numbers we have moved over the last few years from crude and ad hoc assessment procedures to a generally more flexible and refined practice.

The first part of this chapter will consider these developments by sketching the history of Writing's evolution at Crewe and Alsager, showing the institutional and broader ideological pressures that have determined the shape and direction of the subject. The second part will explore our present practices and our proposed developments in assessment, some of which have been noticeably influenced by the demands of the National Curriculum.

Part I

As an early and dependent off-shoot of English in the late 1970s, Writing and its assessment practices reflected the influence of its parent subject –

students wrote essays, sat three-hour written examinations, submitted tutor-set assignments (mainly pastiche and journalistic writing) and produced a limited amount of original work. Over the last decade this has changed substantially. Modes of assessing are far more flexible now, wider in range and objective-related. Students are significant partners in the process; devising particular criteria for particular projects, self-evaluating performance, peer appraising. Our philosophy has been to relate assessment to learning and not to teaching, to develop it as a diagnostic/evaluative process, to soften its judgemental character and to put at the centre of the subject the student's own work.

Talk of 'criteria', 'objective-related' and 'philosophy' suggest carefully planned and systematic structures but the evolution sketched above has been as much casual and opportunistic as deliberate cultivation. Writing, as a new curriculum species, was fortunate in the early days at Crewe and Alsager in finding favourable local conditions and a general beneficial change in climate. Nevertheless a number of tactical, pragmatic and political decisions were made at the very beginning to counter some dangerous assumptions and ignorances about the subject. For instance, so as not to disturb unduly the long settled territories of academic subjects, Writing emerged only slowly from under the influence of its powerful curriculum sponsor – English. In 1982, Writing became a separate autonomous subject, located in humanities, with a subject head, an identified team of tutors, a core of course units and its own budget. Its courses were published in the college compendium, advertised in the prospectus. It was respectable – its origins in English guaranteed that. Gradualism had worked.

Not all sections of the college, nor outside agencies, saw it this way. Was Writing really a legitimate activity in an institution of higher education? Was it academic? This last was an important question in the late 1970s when colleges were trying to establish their credentials and credibility in the higher education sector. Was it a 'subject' at all? Was it not subordinate and marginal, an indulgent activity even, and properly a minor part of options English? Was it not personalizing the curriculum, handing it over to the students, collapsing the academic hegemony that determines curriculum membership and the agenda of knowledge? It was unscientific, untrustworthy, without any apparatus of critical methodology, without a legitimizing tradition. Some treated the subject with lofty paternalism – something for the kids to play with. Others were puzzled. What was it? Literary studies in drag? A few saw it as a dangerous new breed and thought it ought to be chained up to English and not left to roam freely in the wide open spaces of students' experience. Others saw it as a kind of counselling agency, an outreach of student services, offering therapy through confession, release and catharsis.

But perhaps the most persistent doubt and suspicion about Writing as a suitable subject for study in HE hung over the issue of assessment itself. Some validators were puzzled: 'But how do you actually assess it?' Implicit in the interrogative, we felt, were a number of questionable assumptions. Writing, it was being implied, was too subjective, too personal to be measured. How could it submit to the exactitude of grading, to percentaging and classification? It was the old notion that the immeasurable was irrational and so had no place in academic institutions.

Rightly or wrongly we thought the question implied a very limited notion of assessment. It was not to do with grading or ranking performance. It was far more. Assessment was a matter of evaluating, diagnosing and improving performance and only sometimes of converting these processes into numerical or literal equivalents for grading purposes. Assessment was a continuous process, emphatically positive and constructive. And it was not just the privilege and duty of the teacher alone. It was not an imposition by an expert on the uninitiated nor a segregating into good and not so good, but a shared process where the student should be both assessor and assessed, a process primarily concerned with enhancement and development.

Other issues exercised us too. It always seemed illogical to doubt a tutor's ability to assess a student text when for generations other tutors, critics and academics had assessed poems and novels and plays by the good and the great and found no problem ranking such texts in the canonical orders of Eng. Lit. The question too seemed implicitly to devalue the whole process of composition, of creating texts, and to privilege the activity of criticism. It seemed the primal act of creation had been supplanted by the dependent activity of literary analysis and judgement. This, of course, is a distortion of the relationship or interrelationship of creating and the act(s) of literary or textual criticism. The two are one. It is a matter of history and curriculum politics that they have been so separated. In devising our Writing units to balance critical reading with original writing we were hoping to establish an ideal situation where creating and reviewing, revising and evaluating happened at the same time, integrating once again that which in the 'academies' had been separated for too long.

Naturally we argued that this divisiveness did not exist in the other arts, that in the teaching of drama, of the visual and plastic arts, of music, there was a long tradition of critical activity and original composition working side by side. Why not in Writing? Certainly in our arguments we were strident and overly defensive. We may have misunderstood the motives of our questioners. We probably saw as adversarial what in fact were simply the strategies of good advocacy – ways of making us think through our ideas and jolt us out of our complacency.

In disguised forms all these questionings and distortions attended the growth of Writing and determined its character. Our early conservatism in assessment is explicable not just in strategic terms – we wanted to survive and not tread on too many toes – but also as a reaction to the tacit suggestions that Writing was no more than an academic eccentricity. Early discussions about including stylistics and linguistics as major elements in our courses were fuelled by a desire to seem intellectually rigorous and academically worthy.

Similarly our early decision to drop the term 'creative' and insist on 'Writing' as the subject title was only partially based on 'philosophic' grounds, on our views of what Writing was all about. In certain quarters the term 'creative' was disreputable, a synonym for indulgence, for undisciplined and egotistic expression. It was defined, or at least thought of in terms of a simple binary opposition – critical versus creative: good versus bad. *Creative* writing in college was, according to one of our earlier validators, 'no more than the adolescent outpourings of immature minds'. Such a dismissive remark reveals one ideological force shaping the curriculum and one with which Writing at Crewe and Alsager has shadow-boxed for a number of years.

To blunt, even avoid, this kind of antagonism, Writing found a more protected base and sympathetic locale among the expressive arts. Its establishment as a fully-fledged subject area coincided with its inclusion in the Creative Arts degree alongside music, drama, visual arts and dance. From the beginning, its relationship with these subjects highlighted two major aspects of Writing – the notion of *process* and the notion of the *personal*. Within the creative arts, crafting and technical excellence, innovation and originality were the broad criteria of assessment and ones adopted by Writing. In this context they were seen as natural to the subject. No one questioned their aptness and validity. Further, all four expressive arts emphasized process, not product, and learning by doing. Writing was sympathetic to this hieratic approach and has adopted assessment methods pertinent to this developmental character. The degree also acknowledged the centrality of the personal, the student's own experience as creator/ performer. It was this element, the student as 'owner' and definer of the subject that was also central to Writing. Archibald MacLeish has well described the distinctive feature of Writing as 'subject':

> The whole situation of a Writing course is a reversal of the usual academic pattern. Not only is there no subject, there is no content either. Or, more precisely, the content is the work produced by the students. And the relation of the teacher to his [her] students is thus the opposite of the relationship one would expect to find. Ordinarily it is the teacher who knows, the student who learns. Here it is the student who knows, or should, and the teacher who learns or tries to.
>
> (MacLeish 1959)

Both the notions of the personal and the process have important implications for assessment. For instance setting essays – writing on writing – is not necessarily the most effective mode for assessing creative expression. The notebook, the journal, the review might be. However recognizing the primacy of the personal has its problems. For first-year students the lack of determined content and pedagogic authority take some adjusting to, and apprehensiveness about voicing the personal can be creatively debilitating. Our teaching and assessment strategies have had to recognize these important psychological dimensions to the student as writer.

Apart from its supportive positioning in creative arts, Writing found other institutional forces working in its favour. Partnering other subject areas in *combined* degrees meant Writing was implicated in the destiny of those subjects. Writing could not be 'picked off', for instance, without prejudicing recruitment to other areas; no subject in a modular system of combined degrees was free-standing and 'exposed'. To further strengthen its position as a 'new' subject Writing argued forcibly for its inclusion in Initial Teacher Training and by the mid-1980s was offered in four different combined degree programmes as well as in the DipHE.

This diversifying brought its own problems. Writing groups had very mixed populations. For instance, at any one time a workshop class might include creative arts students doing drama, Bachelor of Education students training for teaching, humanities students taking geography. Each of these subgroups had and have very different expectations of assessment. Trainee teachers see it as judgemental, tutor-based and are very aware of grading. Drama students are conscious of a wider range of assessment method. Their experience ranges from collective and oral modes to confessional and fugitive forms like the notebook, journal, review. Humanities students have a more formal perception of assessment based as it is on the essay as the dominant practice.

Diversity also characterized the content of students' work. BEds wrote across a limited range of genre: mainly verse, autobiography and children's stories, whereas creative arts students taking Writing were more willing to experiment and do collaborative work. They found it easier to meet these particular learning objectives. Such students may be further advantaged by recent moves to include oral modes in our range of assessment procedures. The new emphasis on writing for performance will also appeal to students from this area. Even though the subject is pluralist and non-prescriptive, even though students can select from a very broad spectrum of writing modes, it was clear our assessment practice had to be not just sensitive to individual personality but flexible enough to discriminate between the diverse experience of different groupings of students.

Another major influence on the development of Writing was the CNAA. Validators with backgrounds in the various expressive arts were sympathetic to the subject and the first review panel in 1978 unconditionally approved the inclusion of creative writing units in the new Creative Arts degree. The College, too, backed the proposal. It was keen to find a distinctive role in higher education. Recognizing it was unrealistic to try and match the academic profile of university subjects, Crewe and Alsager along with other new colleges of HE opted for a 'distinctive' character to their portfolio. Unusual combinations of subjects, diversity and choice, the offer of new subjects (like Writing), inter-disciplinary and multi-disciplinary work and ease of transfer all freed the curriculum and created a context where innovation and change thrived. In this climate Writing flourished. It was new and different. It offered wide choice and freedom for students to devise their own programmes of work, to negotiate workloads and assessment. It offered new teaching styles and an open learning context.

Part II

This second part looks at present assessment practice in Writing at Crewe and Alsager, quoting extensively from course documentation and the reports of recent assessment working parties. Within the subject we have identified the following eight general principles relating to assessment and these provide the framework for the rest of this chapter.

1 Assessment should serve a number of different purposes

In the following discussion four separate assessment functions are considered:

Diagnostic – where students' strengths and weaknesses are identified.
Evaluative – where the effectiveness of learning and teaching is measured.
Selective – where students' suitability for final year work is determined.
Grading – where students are identified with a particular level of achievement.

2 Assessment should be appropriate: related to subject and unit aims and objectives

The Writing brochure describes the aims of the subject as follows:

> The overall aim of the subject is to provide a lively, sympathetic and creative context in which students can develop as writers. The subject emphasises the inter-relationship of writing and reading. Students, therefore, combine the critical study of the best in contemporary work with their own practice of the craft. The critical study covers units in Years 1 and 2 and students here explore a variety of literary and non-literary texts ranging from documentary to post-modern novel, from feature article to travelogue, radio play to experimental verse.

> The practice of the students' own writing takes place in all years, and the aim is to extend the student's repertoire of writing skills across a wide spectrum of forms and genres and to develop them to professional levels of competence.

> To this end, students must take publication seriously and each year they are required to submit at least three pieces or their equivalent to outside publishers. Though Writing is viewed as a practical activity, students will also consider contemporary theoretical perspectives – such as post-structuralism, feminism etc. – and relate them to their own practice.

The Writing area assumes a particular attitude to composition. Students should see it as a creative process. Writing evolves through progressive stages from drafting, consultation and rehearsed performance, to successive revisions and editing, to final version. The subject is structured to encourage, guide and direct students through this evolution. For their part students should be willing to persevere with the process, be open to new ideas and criticism, and be prepared to experiment.

The content and structure of the subject reflects this central balance between critical reading and the student's original work. The following, from the brochure, briefly describes the shape of the subject.

Content
The two main areas of study are:

the critical study of texts – this takes place in Writer's Craft 1, Writer's Craft 2, Writing Project, Year 3. These units are taught through weekly two-hour classes which involve discussion, practical writing sessions and text-related assignments.

students' own writing – this takes place in Writing 1, Writing 2, Writing 3 and 3A and Writer's Craft 3. These units are taught through tutorial and workshop and involve the practice of writing. The student writes what she wants and submits for assessment a two-part file of finished work: Pt 1 in January and Pt 2 in May. Each part will include details of recent publication.

Structure
The eight *Writing* course units are organised as follows:

Year 1 Writing 1	Writer's Craft 1
Year 2 Writing 2	Writer's Craft 2
Year 3 Writing 3	Writer's Craft 3
Writing 3A	Writer's Project

Each of these areas of study has its own objectives.
Writer's Craft units aim to:

- help students appreciate the full context of Writing, the economic and political, the cultural and social conditions of production
- help students develop a philosophy of writing by presenting different notions about the nature of the writing process and the writer's role and purpose
- introduce students to the best in current practice and relate it to the literary, popular and journalistic traditions of the past
- introduce students to a wide range of literary and non-literary forms and encourage practice in these forms so they extend their repertoire of writing skills and appreciate the different needs of different readerships

- encourage in students the practice of wide and diverse reading and the attainment of high levels of comprehension and interpretative skills
- provide students with a critical terminology and the opportunity to apply it.

Writing 1, 2, 3 and 3A units aim to:

- help students recognise, value and develop their own personal voice in writing
- help develop students' imaginative and creative abilities
- help students develop a feel for language, its possibilities and limitations
- help students become self-critical and self-evaluative
- help students write clear, concise, honest English
- encourage in students a professional sense of procedure, and mss. presentation
- offer students vocationally relevant skills in verbal communication and information technology.

To guarantee that these objectives are achieved we have developed a *variety* of assessment instruments. These include, in Writer's Craft units, short poetry commentaries, the standard essay, self-directed study, mini-files, critical journals and working notebooks, the review, mini-group oral/visual presentations, small group discussions and so on. Students reading out their own work, partner, group and general class debate represent those moments of informal assessment that go on all the time where discussion is a primary teaching method.

In Writing units student performance is assessed in a negotiated context. The student becomes increasingly responsible for her own performance. Tutorials are in essence self-diagnostic and the evaluation/report mechanism (see 3 below) encourages that essential reviewing function of assessment.

3 Assessment should encourage independent and active learning

Writing, as MacLeish has argued, reverses the traditional relationship between teacher and taught. In a real sense students 'own' the subject content. Writing, per se, is student-centred. Though it is easier for Writing than for other subjects to implement this principle it does not happen *sui generis*. It has to be positively and overtly encouraged, especially in the early stages of a taught course. Assessment, then, starts where the students are, and here two crucial issues are involved.

Firstly, the student's profile of development. From year to year student writing differs. In the first year it is often tentative, exploratory and unfinished. Students feel a vague sense of dissatisfaction that nothing has quite worked out. Second-year work is more disciplined and focused. By the third year students have a clear sense of their own voice and have developed well-defined programmes of work. Recognizing this profile, Writing offers maximum tutorial support in the first year and puts the emphasis on the generation of ideas. It aims to build up competence and confidence through workshop sessions and introduces students to as wide a range of writing as early as possible. Assessment, following teaching, stresses originality and innovation in Year 1, but in Years 2 and 3 lays increasing emphasis on formal elements in writing.

A second crucial issue related to student-centred teaching and assessment concerns students' schooling. Many first-year students emerge from 'A' level 'authority' dependent. Secondary education can encourage passivity, the production of 'set' answers, second-guessing what is in Miss's mind. New students often ask what we want them to write. We have devised a number of teaching and assessment strategies to encourage initiative, independence and risk-taking.

In Years 1 and 2 especially we encourage autobiographic writing because we believe it is a rich source of ready material that is unique and individual and where the student is the undisputed expert. Across Years 1 and 2 we introduce students to as wide a range of writing models as possible so no one model becomes the established mode, the 'received' style, to be mimicked for high marks. We stress process not product: the generation and initiation of ideas, their development (revising/drafting) and, finally, the production and evaluation of work. Twice a year in Writing 1 and 2 each student submits a file of original work which includes finished pieces plus all drafts. In addition students have to include an evaluation with Part Two of the file which includes an analysis of how one selected piece progressed from inception to finished state. It is made clear to students that high marks are awarded for intelligent and sensitive revision and not just for a successful final product.

To encourage independence we use the tutorial to invite students to negotiate their own terms for learning. So the student agrees an individual contract with her Writing tutor early in the year. This contract must meet certain broad targets – 9,000 words of finished prose, 35 poems and so on – but the *student* decides *what* she is going to write and agrees a timetable of consultation. Our tutorial strategy is to make the student talk through, 'brain-storm', evaluate, review, edit and revise ideas and early drafts. It is a process of continuous and primarily oral assessment, the agenda determined by the student.

Apart from being an enabler and encourager the tutor in Writing 1, 2 and 3 has a formal assessing role. So the tutor writes a report on each student's file. This report covers three broad areas described by the Joint Writing Assessment working group in the following guidance note:

1 *Identify broad issues* for next year's tutor to discuss. Comments like: 'Discuss other methods of random/chance writing and how to discipline, shape material' is the sort of thing to write here.

2 *Identify strengths or areas of development.* Comments like: 'Strong on dialogue/monologue. Try radio play or interview/profile' would suit.

3 *Identify problem areas.* Comments such as: 'Gender stereotyping in story. Unstable point of view. Wordy/redundant/clichéd writing etc.' might be appropriate.

This report is written on Part 1 of the Writing file submitted in January of each year and provides the basis for a development interview held with each student in February. At this interview students can discuss ways of improving performance, renegotiate their work and contract for the second part of the file submitted in May. The evaluation that accompanies this second part should address the issues raised in the development interview.

4 Students should share in the assessment process

The student as a central agent in the process of assessment has already been described (see 2 and 3 above). In particular students have a major role in achieving the diagnostic and evaluative purposes of assessment. I have outlined how we invite students to plan their own programme of work through the one-to-one tutorial, how intention, method and technique in writing are all matters for tutorial negotiation, and how assessment criteria are agreed on and quantity to be written bartered over. By emphasizing process, the fluid nature of composition, students are forced to be continually critical, self-appraising and evaluative. These perceptions are formalized in their end-of-year evaluation and mid-year development interview.

At present criteria (see 5 below) for the judgemental aspect of assessment, for selecting and grading, are under review by a joint staff/student working group. It is this area of assessment that we feel needs major development. One interesting possibility is collaborative writing. Here teams of up to eight students, working in pairs or 'cells', devise a major writing project. At the planning stage the team generates ideas, selects a topic, devises and writes down the project objectives, agrees organizational and working methods, lists appropriate assessment criteria, agrees a timetable for reporting back, drafting and completing and chooses a final mode of presentation. All this is written up in a project proposal.

A second possibility for development is the more systematic deployment of peer assessment. Under such a system students would write a report on selected work of their colleagues. The report would follow the format of the file reports written by tutors (see 3 above) which emphasize constructive support by highlighting strengths and offering practical ways of improving and developing writing. Of course in devising such reports the reporters will be developing their own critical and evaluative skills.

5   *Assessment should be based on clearly understood criteria*

We have found it very difficult to articulate precise criteria and make distinct what we often treat as intuitive. The following is a descriptive view of criteria related to different kinds of writing and included in our Writing *Handbook* given to all students at the beginning of each year. Following our policy of promoting student-centred learning the *Handbook* asks students to apply the criteria themselves. It also tries to give some idea of how these criteria relate to the grading process:

Writing 1, 2, 3, and 3A
- Ask of a piece of work, do I really believe in this writing? Does it carry conviction? Writing which is flawed in expression, full of bad spelling, fractured syntax and defective style can be powerful writing, the writer's commitment and real feeling showing through the flaws. Top marks go to writing which is both 'felt' and honest and which is well-controlled and free of technical and stylistic defect.
- Self-reflexive forms of writing – diary, journal, autobiography – are good forms to start with. To achieve high marks such work should go beyond self and reflect self in relation to other people and to contemporary society, its ideas, structures, values etc. We feel it is the writer's response and RELATING to her world that is the crucial point. Re-telling is not an adequate response. Writers are not scribes. Writing is RELATING.
- Ask yourself if your work is derivative. Am I just imitating someone else's style? Am I producing 'formula' writing? Mills & Boon, sword and sorcery stuff? Off-the-shelf writing? This sort of fiction does not earn the highest marks.
- Have you edited your work? Have you cut out superfluous words, simplified tortuous sentences, eliminated repetitions and redundancy, substituted concrete for abstract expression, active for passive constructions, fresh expression for cliches? Badly edited work is penalised. Where you have revised and edited credit will be given.
- In verse ask yourself about technique. Have you used a range of rhetorical devices – alliteration, assonance, metaphor, antithesis, rhyme, rhythm, etc? Look at the range of your poetry. Does it cover a wide variety of forms? Lyric, narrative, syllabic? Where there is adventurous handling of techniques, exploration of forms and a wide range of rhetorical devices deployed high marks will be awarded.
- In prose fiction think of the following questions. Is the dialogue convincing? Do the characters live? Or are they stereotypical? Are they varied or monotonously similar? Does the plot hold together? Is the work socially, politically or psychologically aware? What narrative structuring is used? Simple, chronological, or flashback? Is the style distinctive? Is there a clear relationship between form and purpose? Appropriateness of form and style, clarity of purpose, plausibility of

character/dialogue/description and structural inventiveness are some of the criteria by which to assess the quality of prose fiction.
– Journalistic writing should have verve and precision. It should adjust style, angle and subject matter to a target readership. Where there is evidence of research, clear recognition of audience need, carefully structured argument or clear exposition, novel treatment and a succinct style high marks will be awarded. (Writing *Handbook* 1990–1)

6 Assessment should be formal, informal and continuous

A recent Schools Examination and Assessment Council (SEAC) document ably describes the interrelationship of formal and informal assessment:

> Teacher assessment is an integral part of teaching and learning ... Teachers discuss with pupils, guide their work, ask and answer questions, observe, encourage, challenge, help and focus. In addition they mark and review written work ... Through these activities they are continually finding out about their pupils' capabilities and achievements; this knowledge then informs plans for future work. It is a continuous process. It should not be seen as a separate activity ...
> (Schools Examination and Assessment Council 1991)

Our assessment practice has been to encourage the continuous and informal character of the process and to minimize the use of formal instruments of assessing. Only twice a year do students submit their own work for grading, whereas in each of their tri-weekly tutorials their writing is subject to those multiple informal processes described by SEAC.

7 Assessment should be concerned with process as well as product

In a real sense this principle is enclosed within others. To be truly diagnostic and evaluative assessment has to focus on process. Continuous assessment by definition applies to the *process* of learning and it is the focus of student participation in assessment (see 4 and 6 above).

8 Assessment should cover a variety of modes

This principle reflects the multiplicity of factors influencing any one assessment context. No one mode can accommodate the diversity of course material, range of subject objectives and variety of assessment functions. We have tried to develop a *range* of assessing instruments: in any one year a student's portfolio might include some of the following tasks – the essay, a range of original work, tutor-directed assignments (in Writer's Craft units these include travel pieces, a radio play, feature article, short story, autobiographic sketch) poem sequence, journal/notebook, self-directed study, critical evaluation, peer assessment report, group presentation/performance.

Conclusion

In the early days of the modular system uniformity of assessment practice between modules (units) was considered desirable. Each unit of 90 hours had a standard assessment package of two 2,000-word essays or equivalent, plus one three-hour, end-of-year written examination. This comparatively crude structure operated in all units irrespective of its appropriateness. Now assessment is far more differential, sensitive to the nature of the subject and the experience of the student, and matched to the subject's defined learning outcomes. It has grown out of teaching and student learning and is not some externally imposed system.

Since assessment itself is a process and not a product, it will continue to evolve and be responsive to change in both a local and a national context. As access to Higher Education widens student experience and expectation is going to be more diverse. Wider choice, credit accumulation and differential qualifications are all going to affect assessment practice just as the recent demands for more vocationally relevant courses have affected assessment in Humanities and Creative Arts degrees.

It seems, as learning outcomes change and as assessment switches more towards the learner and out of teacher control, that future developments are going to centre on the student. Increasingly the learner is going to have a larger say in determining how her learning is managed. Indeed active participation in the assessment process is itself motivational and an important factor in improving learning.

Reference

MacLeish, Archibald (1959). 'Mostly About Writing', *Harper's Magazine*, October.
SEAC (1991). *Assessment, Key Stage 3*. London, SEAC.

7

The place of creative writing in the development of teachers

Peter Abbs

The development of experience is largely unconscious, subterranean, so that we cannot gauge its progress except once in every five or ten years; but in the meantime the poet must be working; he must be experimenting and trying his technique so that it will be ready, like a well-oiled fire-engine, when the moment comes to strain it to its utmost. The poet who wishes to continue to write poetry must keep in training; and must do this, not by forcing his inspiration, but by good workmanship on a level possible for some hours' work every week of his life.

(T.S. Eliot)

In this chapter I want to examine with examples the practice of writing in the context of the training of English teachers. I have decided to present one term's fairly concentrated work in writing with a Postgraduate Certificate in Education English group at the University of Sussex. I will describe briefly what my intentions were, how the work was structured, what was written and what was claimed, at times, by some of the students. Such descriptions are, of course, inherently problematical. After all, any workshop involves the varied, sometimes volatile, always changing, perceptions of all its members; a workshop group is an extraordinary complex psychic web, impossible to fully represent in words. What I am after in this description is to evoke some feeling of the kind of activity one is seeking to generate, what it can produce in terms of written work and some indication of certain procedures, the practical 'what and how'of a workshop approach to writing. It is not being put forward as an ideal model, but as a modest and incomplete experiment.

My general aim before the course commenced could be defined roughly as follows: I wanted the PGCE English students to have ample experience of writing. I wanted to engender through practice rather than theory a living sense of the process of composition, moving from first hesitant jottings to something like a realization of final form. I wanted them also to have some direct experience of performance (of finding a public voice) and practical criticism. I knew they would all have had years of apprenticeship at writing critical essays, of shaping words to present a discursive argument, and would be masters of the academic apparatus for presenting such arguments, but I suspected that, for the most part, they would be much less at ease with more personal and imaginative forms of expression. It was time for the students to have first-hand experience of the poetic rather than the discursive; experience of thinking through image, narrative, the poetic power of language when it arises out of engaged emotion and imaginative play.

Nietzsche somewhere suggested that in the elevation of conceptual theory lay the roots of nihilism. Was the effect of literary criticism (particularly under the influences of Structuralism and Post-Structuralism) to create a widespread dissociation between the intellectual and the personal? Where there is a near complete division between theoretical abstraction and the psychological life of the one who abstracts, then perhaps the possibility of personal development or of cultural renewal has been rendered all but impossible? This is not an attack on theory, but on theory, spinning theory, spinning theory . . . I hoped the workshops might counter any such dissociation by joining the life of memory, association and feeling to the practical tasks of literary creation and appreciation: by bringing, for example, the material of inherited myth to the material of one's own imagination or by inviting free association and then bringing to the work all the organizing power of an accepted literary convention. Furthermore I wanted the workshops to act as a model for teaching in the comprehensive school where for three days in each week the students would be doing their teaching practice.

The art-critic Anton Ehrenzweig has written:

> The intellect must be enlisted as a potent helper of spontaneity . . . The students must be taught by coercion if necessary – not to wait on their inspiration and rushes of spontaneity, but to work hard at being spontaneous through choosing tasks that cannot be controlled by analytic vision and reasoning alone. We would . . . call on intellect and reason in order to sting into action the powers of the deep.[1]

To develop exercises which promoted imaginative and poetic thinking, to develop mundane methods for releasing imaginative language, to reflect on this process and to consider its educational import: these were the main intentions when the Autumn term started.

In the PGCE university induction week two workshops were set aside for writing. The workshops were to operate from opposite poles. The first was to be open with regard to form and directly personal with regard to content. The second was to be formally prescriptive in that it was to begin as an organized exercise, presenting one poetic form for the structuring of the writing. It was also to be collective in nature in that the work was to be shared and discussed by the group.

Before coming, all the students, as a requirement of the course, had written a fairly sustained piece of discursive autobiography, reflecting on their own education. Now in the very first writing workshop I asked them to select an autobiographical event and to present it not as *abstract* reflection but as embodied symbol, to convey, that is to say, the feel and full specificity of the experience: *how it was.* I read a few pieces of autobiography by comprehensive school pupils and then, without commentary, keeping them in the room, dictatorially set ten minutes of time for the mind and the pen to scratch around in the dry ground for those buried seeds and roots from which the later work might grow. Such prescriptive time-counts can be extremely important in the formal releasing and directing of spontaneity; they seem to create, simultaneously, an inner anxiety and a set context for overcoming that anxiety and producing work that otherwise would never have been created. Ted Hughes has written:

> These artificial limits create a crisis which rouses the brain's resources; the compulsion towards haste overthrows the ordinary precautions, flings everything into top gear, and many things that are casually hidden find themselves rushed into the open. Barriers break down, prisoners come out of their cells.[2]

When the ten minutes were up, I gave 20 minutes for the students to begin the more formal shaping of whatever material they had located. Perhaps, at the end of 20 minutes, they would have, at least, a working first draft if not the completed artefact? At the end of the session I asked them to submit the work, anonymously if they wished, in two days' time, and to add some brief reflections on the actual experience of writing. Here are two of the passages which came in:

First autobiographical passage

This is a moonless night;
Darkness, thick, impenetrable, surrounds me.
Outside the elm trees creak and strain in the rising wind,
Here loneliness and fear pervade the dark stairs.
At the bottom there is a door:
If I can reach it, lift the latch, I will find sanctuary.
Another world, glowing gold,
Tranquil, warm, secure: fire hissing, clock ticking, mother knitting.

Commentary by the author

I wanted to write this episode in prose, but it didn't work – neither does this really, but in some ways it comes closer to my feelings. The language is fairly banal. I can see the scene and feel the emotions in my imagination but I can't convey it in words – the contrast between the dark, forbidding world behind the

*door and the security that the open door promised me, as a small child awoken
on a stormy night.*
(Maureen)

Second autobiographical passage

Sussex Downs

Seen from afar, soft breast-curves rolling,
        tree-filled hollows,
        promising joy;
Encountered closer their pains disclosed
        mean sharp-flint grazed knees,
        wind-whipped wet knickers and cheeks
– Sham comfort
In summer they yield tenderest beauties
        yellow gorse flowers,
        blue fritilleries;
Beauty-eager fingers clutch prickles with the blossoms,
        dead dust on wings,
                life's patterns crumbling.
– Counterfeit beauty.
Lines of young children hold hands on the flint-paths,
        teacher-trailing,
                a chattering throng;
Yet secretly mean fingers pinch, push and scratch,
        cruel words are uttered,
                friendless despair
– Sentimentalised infancy.

Sussex Downs – bleakness-bleak, beauty-bleak, childhood-bleak,
Chalk-hearted, sharp-flinted, cold-fleshed downs
– Archetypal betrayers.

Commentary by the author

*So Wednesday arrived; the subject matter was fine, there was a dominant theme
of alienation in my education. My second school/'home' was Rottingdean, the
Downs unconsciously imprinted on my mind/body, to such a degree that when
I returned to Sussex aged 26 or so I wept quiet tears of suicidal despair on seeing
them – never dreaming why, as I had blocked it all off. Some of the horror peeps
through my poem.*

*But the poem is totally unsatisfactory and incomplete: for lying in one of the tree-
filled clefts of the Downs is the University – my second education. Here the
Downs yielded their treasure without betrayal. Here I conquered the alienation
of my childhood Downs. I wanted to write about the Downs that beat me, and
the Downs I conquered. The polar opposites were too complex for the time allowed. I could only sustain one image, one agony, one emotion in 20 minutes*

or so. There is much to do with the poem – or perhaps with a parallel poem. The problem posed and the intensity of the despair meant I did not try to rework it – I avoided it until handing in time.

As to the session: I found it totally easy to separate myself from my surroundings, to concentrate 100% on the poem. The 'super-ego' was irrelevant. The subject was fine; the structure of the session excellent. I loved the model poems and if I had to imitate the form more-or-less, that didn't worry me; I have so little knowledge of poem forms and no aspiration to originality or genius.

Of the week the poems seem the most meaningful thing at one level. I want to learn to write better and better poetry. I don't want anonymity – I want good, valid criticism. I can't wait for next time.
(Pat)

One of the characteristic rhythms of creativity is to move from *free associative rhythmic play* to the identification *of an emerging pattern* to its *elaboration into a satisfying symbolic form.* Attempting to analyse the elusive nature of the creative act, Einstein wrote:

Taken from a psychological standpoint this combinatory play seems to be the essential feature in productive thinking – before there is any connection with logical construction in words or other kinds of signs which can be communicated to others.

The above-mentioned elements are, in any case, of visual and some of muscular type. *Conventional words or other signs have to be sought for laboriously only in a secondary stage,* when the mentioned associated play is sufficiently established and can be reproduced at will.[3]

Yeats described the same process more imagistically:

Those masterful images because complete
Grew in pure mind but in what began?
A mound of refuse or the sweepings of a street
Old kettles, old bottles and a broken can.[4]

The second workshop was structured to release this rhythmic movement, moving from free combinatory play to conscious construction and, finally, communication. We began with some simple free-association exercises, carefully timed. A word or word cluster was given:

Underground at Rush Hour
Hospital at Midnight
Water
Bride in a Church
Autumnal Tree

In one minute the students had to scribble their immediate associations. Thus within five minutes there was a mass of fairly inchoate material created out of free verbal associative play. The students were then asked to consider their own spontaneous free associations to look not only within one stream but also across streams to see if they could discern any distinct patterns emerging out of the half-random chaos. They were asked to work consciously with these patterns, to see if they could be expanded, to see, as it were, where they would go. For this expansion and elaboration ten minutes were given. At that point I introduced the haiku form with its economic three lines and formal 5/7/5 stress pattern and asked them in a short period of prescribed time to reduce the material they had expanded to a haiku. At the end of the session the small haiku poems were written up anonymously and handed round for a public reading.

Thus in one short session all the stages of art-making had been formally included and, at a simple level, experimentally encountered, from first impulsive jottings ('combinatory play') to conscious shaping into a poetic form, through to performance and communication. Graham in his journal entry for 7 October 1983 wrote up his haiku and commented on the process of composition:

> The pantomime bride
> Bids a forlorn farewell to
> Her summer lovers.

> I'm really very pleased with this. Today was – I think – the first time I had encountered the 'haiku' and having criticised the artificiality of the writing exercise (but not the intention) in the last meeting I was a little suspicious as to how today's exercise would go. However, I can now see more clearly the idea behind such 'control' – that deliberate experimentation with prescribed structures provides the possibility to experience and experiment with different forms of writing; an approach to finding one's own style.

The writing and rendering of haiku in the second workshop suggested a further development in collaborative art-making. Writing about the related Japanese form of *renga* Toyoko Izutsu has pointed out:

> The particular feature of this poetic art, *renga*, is that it is composed not by one poet but by a group of poets gathered together in a party. The units go on being created one by one on the spot and are placed one after another in serial form by the participants taking their turns.

> The starting verse, the very first unit of 5/7/5, assumes technically a particular significance in *renga* so that it is composed usually by an honoured poet in the gathering, known for his conspicuous poetic attainment.

> *Hokku*, the very first verse in the whole *renga* is the only fixed point stably established under the direct control of one individual poet to mark the departure for the whole course of a yet unknown creative voyage, in which functional fluidity and relational mobility play a great

part, preventing any one of the participants from steering its course at will. The participants know only afterwards the whole scope extending from the starting point to the end, recognising it as a wake they themselves have left behind in their group voyage of creation.[5]

In their third workshop (after the students had returned from a longish period in the schools in which they were now placed, for the best part of the year, for three days in each week, with two days at the University) sheets of the haikus, typed up, were handed out. We looked at some translations of Japanese haiku and noted the way they invariably move from a cluster of particular images to hint at a universal, the way in which the concrete object is envisaged as a manifestation of the metaphysical, the way in which also, sometimes, a contradiction is established, an opposition, which is then delicately rooted in the ground of Non-Being:

The sea darkens
The voices of the wild ducks
Are faintly white.

Then I asked the students to take any haiku on the sheet, preferably not their own, and to write, while keeping the structural form of the original, its antithesis in mood and meaning. After ten minutes, the students were asked to exchange with their neighbour the double haiku and now the task was to find, in a third stanza, the resolution, the synthesis.

The pantomime bride
Bids a forlorn farewell to
Her summer lovers.

A summer lover
Preparing his next encore
Grows into autumn.

Off the stage of life
Our dramas enacted
Meet reality.

The brown leaves lie still
Embalmed in the clear water
Reflecting dry death.

The green leaves sparkle
Reflecting in the water
Moist vitality.

Green-striped, muddied brown
Leaves splashed by fungoid fingers
Purity mouldered.

Lindsey, who wrote the resolution of the last sequence wrote in her journal:

Thursday – after a whole week at Seaford Head. It's so strange being back on campus – University life looms large and slightly artificial. It's taxing leaping from one context to another. I feel like a chameleon.

I do enjoy the seminar today though. Peter has had the haiku printed up (my hateful haiku), and we try an experiment. Choosing a haiku, we write an antithesis for it, it is then passed on and someone attempts a reconciliation. Thus, it is a three stage process. Subtly the exercise has prompted us to consider someone else's work critically and also involved us in a cooperative scheme. It really works.

The last three lines are mine and I feel satisfied with them. It falls into place for me. The exercise has a complete feel about it.

Karen, who wrote the original thesis confessed:

What made it difficult for me was resolving somebody else's antithesis and previous thesis. I was amazed to feel a pang of possessiveness as I handed my work to another member of the group.

More than a structural exercise was taking place it would seem!

For the second half of the session we worked with four reproduced self-portraits: two from Stanley Spencer, two from David Bomberg. According to my notes I said something like:

Take one of the pairs. Look at it carefully. You are the person painting. Each stroke expresses a disposition, a moment of declaration, of un-ease, of self-discovery. Express the movement of the mind in words as the portrait is painted. Now look at the second painting. Do the same. Now finally see these immediate rough jottings as the material for a unified piece of writing.

Lindsey's reaction to this command was interesting in the light of Ehrenzweig's comment on 'work[ing] hard at being spontaneous'. Lindsey wrote in her journal:

Peter hands us a choice of self-portraits and we are to write in whatever form we wish feelings and thoughts that occur to us when we reflect on them. I feel rebellious. I don't like the pictures. They do nothing for me. However I mull over them and suddenly almost miraculously I'm fascinated and threads start un-winding in my mind zig zagged and haywire. It's like a giant puzzle and it excites me.

It may be that at times the material creates the mood and sets the mind off from its peripheral preoccupations into something deeper. I am sure, as I will show later, this is certainly often the case reworking mythical material. Something more than 'self-expression' takes place in such unexpected encounters from which conversations grow.

This was Frank's work in response to the two portraits by Stanley Spencer:

Two Pictures

I

Black on white. Strange how the face of youth
Should look so like a fingerprint,
A mass of whorls and eddies on the cheek.
An assertion of identity, the ink
Rocking weightily downwards
On lip and jawbone. Round the neck
A loose fold, like a rope,
Knotted. The glint of his reflection
Caught only on the hair
(it will grow in the coffin); none in the eyes.
The stare says: 'Mine is the confidence
Of the innocent, and the resignation
Of the condemned man.' Entered into freely.

This the newly-stamped, a seal of approval.

II

Then, so many years later, another identity parade.
Again the paper is saturated, again
The pressure evenly applied. Yet
Here the pattern has been rubbed away
As if glasspapered; only the eyes
Are polished by the process, shrunken but magnified
Under dead lenses. At the crown
A crop of autumn flax, bent double
Before it breaks the skin, waits on the sickle.
Each line offers over our heads
The stillness of the solitary: a mute lip worn
Like a convict suit, the jaw locked around it.
And that open throat, yielding its scars,
Is the most and least human part,
A withered root for the head.

Now he is released into silence;
Once hung already.

In his journal, Frank commented:

Today's writing: the poems from portraits. I recognised the Stanley Spencer, but tried not to let it interfere with my perceptions. Unfortunately I've lost my original notes from which Two Pictures was drawn: but there is a first and second draft before the 'finished' thing. I was pleased (and amazed) at the way the poem emerged (so quickly) from the notes – in the end, it took maybe a couple of hours to reach its typed state. It's the first substantial piece of writing that I've done in a few years – that, in itself, is enough justification (from my selfish point of view) for the practical component of these workshops.

One note about it: Graham criticised what he felt was the overplaying of the scarf-as-rope motif. However, much of my thinking about the art-as-hanging theme came from the fact that the second picture of Spencer bears (to me) an uncanny resemblance to John 'Babbacombe' Lea, the man who was 'hung' three times in 1913, commuted to life imprisonment. Hence the 'art' = 'death' ('a living death') idea playing through the poem, and made explicit at the end.

A question: how effective/valid would the poem be without the pictures to accompany it?

I began the next workshop by asking the group to respond immediately and imaginally to the following propositions:

On the horizon a city burns
The jester looks out from a pack of cards
The painter faces a blank canvas
Sadness came
The old woman considered her death
Love entered

Some of the responses were as follows:

On the horizon a city burns
A scarlet sunset killing the day

On the horizon a city burns
A lion roars in its cage

Love entered
Celestial light spilling from the sun

Love entered
Like a kingfisher dipping the surface of a tranquil stream

The old woman considered her death
A knot in the thread, her sampler finished

The painter faces the blank canvas
Pondering a field of perfect snow

Sadness came
The noise of the last train over the bridge

The jester looks out from a pack of cards
Leering at the slow shuffle of humanity

As with many of the imagist poets, it was discovered that the easiest movement was from the abstract or general to the specific and imaginal (of Ezra Pound's 'faces on the underground/petals on a wet black bough' or T.E. Hulme's 'Sounds fluttered/like bats in the dark'). Thus the statement 'love entered' was easier to complement with an image than the already imagistically suggestive 'the jester looks out from a pack of cards'.

The students were then asked to take the ones they felt they could develop further. These were some of the results:

Love entered
An Astaire pirouette across marble flights
that laced me in the orbit
Of your dancing passions.

Sadness came
Like dipping leaves in a pool
One by one.

The old woman considered her death
The dust and disappointment of years
Twinkled in the evening sunlight
Then fell grey, shrouding the darkening room
Muffling her gentle sighs.

A great way of generating creative play with language, wrote Kevin in his journal, but Graham's commentary was, in the light of my earlier remarks about the reciprocal relationship between image and emotion, particularly revealing;

> *This was an interesting exercise and one which I look forward to trying with a class (I think my top-band 3rd years could handle this well). I think this exercise worked ultimately for me because I tend to write in sharp, dense images. But I find it so difficult to begin with – I really didn't feel that I got on with the first three initial impulses. I must admit that I didn't feel particularly interested at the start of yesterday's lesson anyway (we all have our off days). But it is very interesting how I was suddenly able to synthesise the fourth and sixth ideas. All of a sudden these ideas struck a very personal (and emotional) note in me, and the exercise suddenly took on a very intense and significant meaning, emotionally rather than intellectually.*

> *Love entered*
> *The visitor left her calling card*
> *You took away my life in your suitcase.*

> *I'm proud of that poem; it may be 'one from the heart' but I think it is direct and unequivocal in its effect as the (really good, even though I say so myself) image of the first two lines is dramatically realised in the final line. I wasn't too sure about reading it out in class – the creation of it and seeing it on the page in front of me really shook me up – but I'm glad I did . . . Apart from the educational significance of the exercise it was a great opportunity for me to resolve some feelings – thank you!*

For the next workshop I distributed round the room a mass of photographs. The students were invited to select one and use it, in whatever way seemed 'right', as a starting-point for their own writing. I followed this workshop a week later with mythical images. I selected some striking images from the strange myth of Perseus and Medusa. Then I asked the students to consider ways in which the images could be developed or adapted in terms of their own experience and our own age. In his book *The Witness of Poetry* Czeslaw Milosz has pointed out the advantages of using such material:

> Perhaps there is a good craftsman concealed in
> every poet who dreams about a material already
> ordered, with ready-made comparisons and metaphors
> endowed with nearly archetypal effectiveness and,
> for that reason, universally accepted; what remains
> then is to work on chiselling the language.[6]

Milosz is surely right in saying that the writer in using myth can concentrate more easily on style knowing that the given story possesses some kind of universality. But it is also true that mythological symbols possess a great and multifarious energy and can excite the imagination to extend or, in some minor or major way, alter their references and so create new meanings yet still mythically charged. In this way the great myths can be endlessly recreated to meet personal and collective needs. Does Prometheus become Frankenstein at the beginning of the nineteenth century and Pincher Martin in the middle of the twentieth century?

In the workshop I was stumbling towards some kind of concentrated exercise in which powerful mythical images could be contemplated and elaborated. I read twice a number of loosely related passages about Perseus journey, his shield, Medusa, the snakes, the power of Perseus with the head of Medusa to turn others to stone. The first time I asked them just to listen; the second time to make notes about any particular image which struck them. Then I asked them to engage with and amplify their notes, and to see what happened.

Alan scrawled down the memory of a disturbing experience while on a bus journey:

> *I knew that if I only stared forwards, out into the world, I should remain free. Hot irons, red beams were burning in straight parallel lines through my head, carving out my head like sculpture, taking on my gaze and making it her own. There was no question of leaving the bus, for I was on a journey. A woman, behind me on a bus, looking through my head and controlling my eyes.*

> *I knew I must not turn my head because if I only glimpsed her look then I would do all she commanded. From the point of sight I would be her own body, an extension, a strange limb whose movement could be traced purely to her eyes. I looked up into the night sky, now black and coagulated and I saw it was no longer the sky of my words, the movements of my possibilities but had become a black hood, carefully and eternally her shadow.*

Alan then brought the experience and the ancient myth together in the following notes towards a poem:

Medusa

I knew that you could only take my self
if you could match my gaze with yours,
map onto my look, onto my making
and make them your command.

I knew that if I turned to face your self
It would be war and I the loser,
For I have no shield
or mirror to protect me.

Only air between us,
egg thin light shattered
penetrating beams of sight
search my head,
carving thoughts-like-sculptures
turned to stone;

swallowed in its mist
your making me an Other
the body of a dead man.

Alan's response to the mythological images brings out in dramatic form the
encounter between personal experience and inherited mythic symbolism.
In his journal Alan wrote:

*The Medusa story has never been one which has interested me in any way in
the past, but in this seminar I suddenly cottoned on to something about it – the
idea of the Other, the 'look' – which gave me some insight into why it remains
such a powerful myth.*

*The force of the story derives, I feel, from the sense in which it reifies 'the look',
makes the existence of one's self contingent upon the creative minds of other
'lookers'.*

*Also, the way in which Perseus then goes on, after slaying Medusa, to have such
total power, is frightening... This idea springs mostly, for myself, from the
writing of Sartre on others, on being-in-itself and being-for-itself.*

*I then wanted to use the experience which I once had of being in a bus and of
feeling the stare of the woman behind me penetrating through the back of my
head, tempting and almost seducing me to turn around and to meet her eyes.
But the atmosphere of the seminar was a difficult one in which to control and
contain in any poem a sense of something so fundamental, and essentially
disturbing... Still, it was good for me because it connected this important
notion to a myth which had been hitherto remote and opaque to me.*

For Maureen a story was suggested:

A man marries the sort of woman who freezes all feeling in those around her, although like Medusa she had once been a human being. It is a long journey of realisation for the man that people turn to stone at his wife's presence and he feels that together they live 'isolated at the end of the world'. The only way he can manage to keep living with her is by not looking directly at her but by holding an image in his mind of the way he remembers her when they first met. He decides that carrying this memory in his mind he will defeat her, and while she lies sleeping, kills her and cuts off her head. But although he buries the body he keeps the head – there is still a terrible fascination in it even after death. Gradually as he lives with his guilty secret, he becomes aware that the strange power of the head has passed to him: he becomes hard, shrivelled, with the force to freeze others. People's reactions change towards him: from being a nonentity he becomes respected and feared, from being weak he enjoys power, but from being warm and alive he becomes dried, frozen himself, unable to feel, cast in stone. The head has become a curse as well as a power.

Maureen wrote the opening paragraph to the story in the workshop:

Medusa

The visitor's voice trailed off into cold silence; his body felt hollow, lifeless, and yet his feet appeared to have grown steel claws which fastened him to the ground preventing escape. The sudden slamming of the door shut the face from his sight and spelt his release. Inside the house the husband listened to the footsteps fade into the distance. He carefully averted his eyes as the woman swept past him, knowing the power of that terrible face: the hair barbed and fortified, the mouth a slash in frozen marble and the eyes, above all the eyes, pitiless diamond lozenges which spoke only death. It had not always been thus. Once long ago she had been a human being, but since that time they had travelled a great distance together, almost it seemed to the end of the world.

In her journal she commented as follows:

I had time only to make a beginning on actually telling the tale. I was quite pleased with my introduction for the story and the first few lines came to me fairly easily. I wished very much that there was time for us to complete projects like this – far more satisfying than preparing endless lesson plans. This is what I wrote as my introduction to what looks as if it could be classified as a 'horror' story.

I hope to have given some conception of a practical workshop approach to English. The aim was to promote creativity in a disciplined context working in the manner of the art, drama and dance teacher. Although at the end of the last workshop the possibility of story writing was beginning to emerge, most of the writing was confined to poetic forms.

What, then, was the connection between the workshops described and the students' teaching in the classroom? What I was trying to present was a way of working which (with necessary modifications) could be eventually tried out in the classroom. I was out to offer an experience which could be slowly integrated by the PGCE students and extended, by degrees, to their teaching practice. The journals of the students reflected on this connection, sometimes with a certain unease, sometimes with a new angle of perception (as in Fiona's remarks about 'precis' below), sometimes with a great sense of identification and excitement. Here are some characteristic reflections:

Imagistic work. Very satisfying to play with oneself (myself) – probably very interesting as a basis for school work; the big question being the age groups with which this would be constructive to try. My sureness of touch with regard to the vastly differing cognitive abilities of different age groups, particularly in relation to 2nd and 3rd years, is definitely not yet adequate to introduce these sorts of 'stimuli' – it may well be . . . and I certainly don't feel up to effectively communicating the nature of the activity yet. But . . . Definitely a great way of generating creative play with language though.
(Graham)

I liked the idea of working up to a small finished idea through the attempt to complement and amplify initial images. I would very much like to use this approach in class as I think I would probably have the right balance between structure and freedom to allow the children to feel absorbed and yet free to write as they pleased.
(Alan)

I have used haiku in the classroom on several occasions. Not always successful, but the students seem to enjoy working with the form. With one third year class I arranged for them to do paintings in their art lessons so that the haikus could be superimposed. The art teacher responded well and combined the exercise with the experiment of colour. The paintings are nearly finished and when mounted they should look quite impressive.
(Susan)

If a teacher is going to engage his/her classes in this activity at all (apart from perhaps once or twice a year) then it must be known intimately by that teacher at first hand. To a teacher who never writes him/herself, or who has never written as an adult, I shouldn't imagine that creative writing 'enters into it' at all.
(Kevin)

Thinking today about the fact that I was made to do so much precis at school it has now occurred to me that writing poetry, if an amount of discipline and thought is applied in its process could be as 'beneficial' as precis in developing a concise but at the same time evocative picture or presentation of an original idea. By constantly refining our words and phrases for the desired effect we are

exerting as much self-discipline as if we were required to reduce a page to 150 words. A ridiculous reduction of the purpose of poetry? Maybe an argument to counter the 'free expression as catharsis' view of writing.
(Fiona)

The purpose of our doing this sort of thing is that it will give us a better idea of what we want from the children and of what we want them to get from the exercise. Not the least of which is self value for by encouraging children to speak about themselves you are tacitly informing them that they are important. This is not to be under-estimated when you remember that the examination system holds people to be important only in so far as they are capable of attaining 'O' and 'A' levels.
(Garry)

I have quoted at some length so as to bring out the different ways in which a very strong connection *was* made between the university workshop and the school classroom. Alan's remark about getting 'the right balance between structure and freedom to allow the children to feel absorbed and yet free to write as they pleased' goes to the heart of the matter and also shows the internalization of our common workshop practice into his teaching. This is exactly what one is hoping will take place, that the students will transfer their experience of the creative discipline of imaginative writing within a literary tradition to their own developing teaching. Other related university work, such as the discussion of lesson plans, the bringing in of creative work from the classroom for evaluation and the critical and open examination of the best ways of teaching literature at different levels, further extends and strengthens this crucial connection.

The workshops I have described were limited in range and took place over one Autumn term. However any adequate creative course for PGCE English students would have to include, *at least*, the informal awareness of many genres and modes of literary expression including, not only poetry and myth (vital as these are), but also the story and novel; autobiography, diary and journal; play-script and documentary; essay and sketch; as well as some exploration of film, video, radio and television. This is a daunting agenda. With regard to the forms of poetry and narrative, I have tried recently (with John Richardson)[7] to provide a comprehensive programme built on the three principles of creative expression, critical awareness and a living knowledge of the whole tradition, from Sappho to Plath, from Homer to – Hughes? But more important than the programme (which must always remain radically incomplete) is an awareness of the philosophical principles on which such work is based. As this is, to some extent, a personal matter I would like to conclude by describing what lies at the centre of my own practice.

I see human beings as creative agents who, through contact with the best elements of a living culture, and through their own expressive and imaginative acts, can develop lives of inner significance and communal value. In *political terms*, it is a matter of people possessing their lives and securing the power and means to participate in a cultural democracy. In *educational terms*, it is a matter of individuals being continually open to further truths, further configurations of meaning discovered either through direct creative work or through a kind of submission to the power of other imaginative work in the literary tradition. In *spiritual terms* it concerns a sense of interior trans-cendence impossible to describe fully but which is often sensed in the engaged acts of imaginative writing or creative performance. It takes the form of a sensation of being 'there' in some transpersonal space resonant with silent meaning. These three categories of concern, political, educa-tional and spiritual, are not, of course, mutually exclusive or in any kind of competition. They are all, in their manifold implications, necessary to any concept of human wholeness, whether personal or communal; and on their difficult and exacting integration must, surely, depend the survival of our culture and our species.

I am not saying that all PGCE English programmes must have such a philosophy to be 'successful'. I am saying, though, that I think these values underlie my own practice and, furthermore, that under *any programme* there must always lie some kind of philosophy, which should be articulated and considered. We need to know what that philosophy is, and why it matters. I have thus concluded a very pragmatic account of a limited number of writing workshops in a very un-English way: I have put my philosophical cards face-up on the table and leave it to my readers to judge for themselves.

Notes

1 Anton Ehrenzweig, *The Psycho-Analysis of Artistic Vision and Meaning* (London, Routledge and Kegan Paul, 1953).
2 Ted Hughes, *Poetry in the Making* (London, Faber and Faber, 1967).
3 Einstein, quoted in Arthur Koestler, *The Act of Creation* (London, Picador, 1966).
4 W.B. Yeats, from 'The Circus Animals' Desertion', in *Collected Poems* (London, Macmillan, 1963).
5 Toyoko Izutsu, 'An Aspect of Haiku Aesthetics', in *Temenos*, (2), 1982.
6 Czeslaw Milosz, in *The Witness of Poetry* (Harvard, Harvard University Press, 1983).
7 See Peter Abbs and John Richardson, *The Forms of Narrative* and *The Forms of Poetry* (Cambridge, Cambridge University Press, 1990).

8

Teaching writing at 'A' level

Nick Rogers

At school I loved writing stories and poems and until I was about 15 my enthusiasm was warmly encouraged by my teachers. After that age it gradually became clear that my own attempts to write creatively were no longer considered relevant to the serious study of English. As 'A' level students we learned that our aims were to be able to write a good literary essay and to refine our sensibilities through appreciation of the great writers of the past, but not, emphatically not, to try to emulate those writers. If one did have the presumption to continue to try to write creatively it was best to keep quiet about it and only share the secret with one's closest friends. I found a similar attitude to students' creative writing when I went on to read for a degree in English. I remember, both at 'A' level and at degree level, teachers vaguely alluding to mysterious creative writing options which we were rapidly advised not to consider unless we were very confident of our talent. Unsurprisingly no one I knew ever attempted them. It was not that my teachers were hostile to creative writing. I am sure that if I had had the nerve to broach the subject of my own writing they would have been interested and no doubt very helpful. The problem was that there was no room for it in the work we did in English.

It seems that this state of affairs is at last beginning to change. Creative writing is still the mainstay of English up to the age of 15 and now forms a significant part of the work for GCSE. It is also now possible to take courses in writing at degree and postgraduate level and there are classes available in further and adult education. In spite of this the traditional 'A' level English Literature syllabus has not changed greatly since I took it in

1968. It still consists mainly of the study of set texts with assessment based on literary essays done in examination conditions. However a number of alternative 'A' level syllabuses have been introduced over the past decade which are beginning to change the picture a little. It is the impact of these new syllabuses on the practice of teaching at this level which I want to consider in this chapter.

The development of alternatives to the traditional 'A' level English Literature examination has generally included the introduction of some form of course work and boards such as the Joint Matriculation Board (JMB) are now offering students an opportunity to submit some of their own creative writing as an integral part of their course work rather than as as an optional additional paper. The students' own writing will typically form part of a folder of work which is assessed and added to the results of their final examination. This course work element may be located in a variety of contexts. Firstly it may have been introduced as an extension of a syllabus which still consists predominantly of a study of literary texts. The JMB's English Literature syllabus C for example, requires candidates to submit a course work file including a piece of 'composition'.[1] Secondly a folder of the students' original writing also forms an integral part of the JMB English Language syllabus, a syllabus based predominantly on the study of language in which the study of literary texts plays only a small part. Students are required to produce three pieces of writing intended to 'persuade, inform, instruct or entertain'.[2] The Associated Examination Board (AEB) English Language and Literature syllabus 623 also aims to promote 'the ability to write accurately, intelligibly and consistently for different purposes', but this ability is tested in the form of a timed examination, not through course work.[3] In addition to these examples there are also creative writing elements in several 'AS' level syllabuses such as those offered by the AEB, the London Board (which includes an optional section on writing short stories)[4] and the Oxford and Cambridge Board's English Language 'AS' syllabus which asks for 'sustained original writing'.[5] So creative writing might be done in the context of a study of literary texts, or a study of language, or as part of a combined course. In future, however, movements towards the modularization of 'A' level may mean that students will increasingly combine elements of language and literature syllabuses. In all cases the weighting of the syllabus means that there is quite a severe restriction in the amount of time that can be made available to help students to develop their own writing. (The number of marks available for the creative writing component in the syllabuses mentioned above varies, but the largest proportion is the 25 per cent allocated for original writing by the JMB English Language syllabus.)

There are important differences in the kind of writing that is likely to be produced in these different contexts and these differences are likely to persist for some time, even with the advent of modularization. Any writing done as part of a literature-based course is likely to be heavily influenced by the models of 'good literature' which are implicitly being offered else-where on the course. Students are likely to transfer the concept of what is valuable in literature, learned in the study of set texts, to their own writing. Thus they may be expected to aim at producing pieces of high art, an endeavour which is viewed as being an end in itself. The genres which are attempted will invariably be those associated with literature, such as short stories, poetry, essays and occasionally plays. The writer will be under no obligation to define his intended readership. On the other hand, writing done in the context of a language-based course will be less influenced by literary models and may well be based on journalistic, popular or trans-actional models. The JMB English Language syllabus requires candidates to produce a folder of three pieces of writing differentiated according to purpose and each with a clearly defined audience. The criterion which students are encouraged to use to evaluate their work is functional: 'will it do the job?' Certainly students of English Language will submit literary genres such as stories, plays and poetry, but these must have a specified purpose, usually 'to entertain', and they will generally only count for one-third of the folder, unless of course they decide to use a literary genre to do something other than to entertain (for example a student writing a piece which is intended to explain the life cycle of a ladybird to eight-year-olds might decide to do it in the form of a short story).

Each of these contexts contains pitfalls for the apprentice writer which need to be guarded against. Writing done as part of a literature course is at risk of turning out to be pretentious and overwritten. Students often wish to try out a variety of literary techniques as they become aware of them, an activity which is useful and helpful to their understanding of literature, but which can result in using only partially understood literary devices for their own sake – the creative equivalent of the weak student who analyses a piece of poetry by listing metaphors and examples of onomatopoeia. Obviously such writing results from a misunderstanding of what literature is and how it works but this is not uncommon at this level. There will tend to be a reluctance to use the language which the student is most familiar with and students may need to be reminded of the validity of their own language and indeed of their own experience.

The danger of writing done in the context of a language course is at the opposite extreme. Some students may avoid challenging tasks and opt for purposes and audiences that demand little in terms of stylistic range or inventiveness. Unless they are made aware of the complex, multi-faceted nature of most texts, they may adopt a very simplistic notion of transac-tional writing and produce bland, monotonous work in a limited register.

Athough these new developments have proved extremely popular with students they have also provided a challenge to many teachers who have not previously had to teach creative writing at this level. The problem facing teachers is how to use the limited amount of time effectively to ensure that students are able to show a development beyond GCSE.

The first question we need to consider when we start a course of writing at 'A' level is what exactly are we aiming for? Obviously not literary master-pieces or works of earth-shattering profundity. We are dealing with students who are usually relatively inexperienced in the world of 'adult' writing and who are coping with quite a heavy academic commitment. They are ap-prentice writers and they need to learn the basic skills of the craft. Students often write very well at GCSE but we need to show a clear development. What are we looking for at 'A' level which we do not expect at GCSE? Well certainly a greater degree of maturity, shown perhaps by choice of subject matter, treatment of subject matter and by the writer showing an awareness of the complexities of adult life. The development here will be helped by sensitive guidance and discussion but to some extent will occur naturally. Another area in which we can expect to see a development beyond GCSE, and one which generally requires more direct intervention and a well thought out teaching strategy, is the student's level of consciousness about the writing process. We want them to actively consider alternative strategies in their writing, to be aware of the choices they are making and to be able to ex-plain, as far as possible, why they made these choices. Finally we want them to develop the capacity to evaluate their own writing in a constructive way. We want them to be able to assess clearly what they have achieved and also recognize what they have not yet mastered, what does not yet work. As a teacher I am concerned with moving the students from a state in which they are producing 'school' writing, often bearing only a passing similarity to any writing in the world outside school, for which the primary audience is still generally the teacher, to a state in which they are able to identify the needs of a range of audiences and call upon a variety of strategies to meet these needs. In other words they should be well on their way to becoming independent writers.

A number of strategies have been developed to set students on this path, to help them begin to become independent, self-aware and self-critical writers. I shall outline some of them below. It is important, as I have suggested, to begin to get students to conceive of an audience wider than the teacher. There are various ways of doing this and the search for 'real' audiences is a challenge to teachers of writing at every level. Clearly one possibility is that the teaching group itself can be turned into an audience and can give feedback to the individual members. However they will need to develop their skills as critics first. I have found this 'workshop' approach unproductive if participants have not yet learned to receive and give criti-cism. It is not a good idea to ask a student to read their anguished poems of loneliness and despair to a group of their peers with no preparation. An atmosphere of trust needs to be established. I would begin first with some fairly short extracts from established writers, not exclusively 'literary', perhaps some 'popular' fiction set against something regarded as 'classic'. I have found Barbara Cartland enormous fun to study in the classroom and very productive when compared with D.H. Lawrence or Jane Austen. Extracts from Enid Blyton might be set beside William Golding, James Herbert beside Edgar Allan Poe.

Part of the spin-off from using extracts like these is the opportunity it gives to examine the borderline between what is regarded as 'great literature' and what is regarded as 'popular fiction', an activity valuable for students taking either the literature or the language syllabuses. I would use short extracts without identifying the source so that there are no preconceptions and the aim would be for the students to respond honestly to the writing. After discussion, the next stage would be to identify the stylistic features of the extracts. Useful questions are: What kind of language is being used? Where does it come from? Are there any distinctive sentence structures being used? If there is any dialogue, who is allowed to say what? What is the narrator's role? Finally an invitation to carry on the extract imitating the style will invariably produce writing which reproduces some of these features which can then be read out and discussed by the group in terms of how accurately it reproduces the style of the original. The advantage of this way of beginning a workshop approach is that it eases students into their role as 'audience' in a non-threatening way. Because the criteria are stylistic the discussion will tend to be about particular words and phrases: Why does that word seem 'wrong' for that writer? What is it about that sentence that makes it seem inappropriate? The students will be more able to distance themselves from what they have written and consider alternatives than they would be if their 'own' writing was at stake.

The next step would be to do a bit of style swapping. Again this is something students enjoy and which, by still protecting them from the need to invest much personally or to generate a completely 'new' piece of writing, enables them to begin to focus on making choices at the stylistic level. Style swapping involves rewriting texts in the style of another writer, so students might take the example quoted above and rewrite a passage from Barbara Cartland in the style of D.H. Lawrence and vice versa. Again these exercises can be read out and enjoyed and discussed. Another productive activity is to invite students to rewrite familiar fairy stories in the style of a well known popular writer. These exercises in pastiche and parody are helpful because they highlight stylistic choices, they provide the student with a structure and a specific aim so they feel safe and they provide useful non-threatening material with which the group can begin to function as a workshop providing constructive feedback to its members. If, however, the group is still not functioning as a supportive but discriminating 'ear' for members' work, I have found that it sometimes helps to ask the group to provide the feedback in writing. Each piece of work in first draft form is simply passed around the group with a sheet for comments, with the invitation to make comments as specific as possible. At the end of the session each member of the group will have a sheet of written responses to her work and she can then go away and redraft. It is important that the teacher joins in these exercises and offers her work for comment in the same way as the students.

Once the group has begun to function as a workshop it is important to keep the momentum going by regular sessions which combine writing, feedback and redrafting. There are a vast number of 'writing games' which are enjoyable to play and which help focus students' attention on a particular aspect of the craft. Whilst the actual writing produced in these sessions is, or should be, very brief (because the focus is narrow and specific) the work should not be thrown away but kept in a file. Partly this is because the writing may be used by students as a starting-point for longer pieces of course work, and partly because it provides a record of the individual's development and can be a useful reference document when course work proper begins and the tutor needs to talk individually with the student about this writing. Most teachers of writing have their own repertoire of writing games and are frequently devising new ones. They seem to me to fall into two broad categories. Firstly there are those which focus on a specific literary technique. These are rather like exercises in music in that they artificially separate a technique from the whole so that it can be practised independently. However they are unlike musical exercises in that they are not repeated regularly to produce fluency, but are intended to increase the range of strategies open to the apprentice writer. Awareness of these strategies is then reinforced by the student's own reading. For example, one might experiment with person and tense to see what different effects can be achieved. One way to do this is to ask the students to produce a few paragraphs of straightforward narrative. It may be helpful to suggest some ingredients such as a character, a place, a time of day. It is likely that when the narratives are read out all of them will be in a form of past tense and that they will be written in the first or third person. The next step would be to consider some of the alternatives which could have been used and then to choose one of the narratives to work on further. If copies can be made at this point it is a great help, otherwise the story must be reread aloud a couple of times. The tutor then allocates variations of person and tense to the members of the group, so for example one person will have the job of rewriting a third-person story in the first person, another will experiment perhaps with the second person, somebody else may try first-person present tense, another future. Further variations might involve an observing narrator who is intensely jealous or perhaps afraid of the main character. The narrator must say nothing about themselves but convey the jealousy or fear in the way the story is told. When all these variations are read out the effects on the reader of each one can be the subject of discussion. A session like this can usefully be followed up by studying a few short stories specifically chosen to show how writers exploit some of these possibilities.

Other fruitful areas for exploration and experiment are dialogue, characterization and rhyme and metre. One exercise I like which I think originated with W.H. Auden consists of asking the group to write a description of a person or a place they know well and to make it as vivid as possible without using any adjectives. This generally has the effect of forcing the writer to use verbs much more inventively than usual and it often gives the description a solidity which is very effective. It is important, I think, very early on to make students aware of the positive effects of careful trimming and pruning. In fact the creative potential of leaving things out is often a revelation to apprentice writers. Many students start their 'A' level course thinking the more they write the better, just as they often think the longer the word they use the better, and it is often with a sense of liberation that they begin to realize that leaving things out can greatly improve a piece of writing, or that a simpler word can be far more effective. Games and exercises which require students to reduce their own writing by a third and then again by another third are helpful. Students could be asked to 'reduce' each other's work by a set amount and different versions could be discussed. Such exercises can also provide evidence of summary skills which is a required component of the AEB course work file. Similarly many students at this level try and explain too much. They may, for example, ruin a perfectly good dramatic moment in a story by telling the reader too much about what the characters are feeling rather than letting her respond imaginatively to the situation. This overwriting is often evident at the end of stories. Games which involve 'finishing' a narrative at different points can be useful in highlighting this problem, as indeed can a study of the kind of advertisements which force the reader or viewer to decode the message themselves.

The second kind of writing exercise involves generating material for writing. While I have described students as 'apprentice writers' and implied a view of writing as a craft that can be learned, it also seems to me to be true that a good writer needs something else, something which cannot be taught like other skills. Gertrude Stein talked about 'a sudden creative recognition',[6] by which I take her to mean the act of seeing connections, in the flotsam and jetsam of everyday life and of the unconscious, which have the potential to be transformed into a piece of creative writing. Seamus Heaney compares what he calls 'technique' (as opposed to 'craft') to the practice of water divining and says, 'The crucial action is pre-verbal, to be able to allow the first alertness or come-hither, sensed in a blurred or incomplete way, to dilate and approach as a thought or a theme or a phrase.'[7] This ability seems to be partly to do with putting the conscious mind 'on hold' temporarily and being open to other elements and then following our instinct for what 'seems right'. Some writing exercises can help students to 'tune in' to this level of perception. They can introduce them to the possibilities of deriving ideas from improvization, from dreams and from serendipity. Simply asking the students to write fast and continuously to a set time limit can be a useful 'unblocking' mechanism and an effective way of cheating the 'inner censor', although it should be made clear to the group that students will not be asked to read out work done in these conditions to the rest of the group. An experiment with William Burroughs's cut-up technique, where bits of text are haphazardly cut up and stuck together in a random order, can intrigue students and throw up startling and resonant images which may later be incorporated into their writing. Similarly the kind of drama exercises described in Keith Johnstone's excellent *Impro* can easily be adapted for a creative writing class and if handled carefully can produce some profound and challenging material.[8] There are various collaborative writing exercises which also introduce an element of unpredictability and sometimes release images of surprising power. For example, words and phrases can be generated collectively in response to a particular image on an overhead projector. The group can then work in twos or threes to turn these isolated words and phrases into a poem or a short piece of prose. A more structured form of collaborative writing would be creating *renga*, or chains of haiku, with a common theme. Like work springing from imitation and parody, collaborative writing has the advantage of being easier for an inexperienced group to discuss critically because it is not 'owned' by a single individual. Exercises of this kind help students to develop a sense of writing as a delicate balance between tight control (craft) and happy coincidence.

Another area in which writing games can help in generating material is in demonstrating the validity of the student's own experience and language. Frequently students on both 'A' level language and literature courses fail to use the richest and nearest potential resource for ideas when they start to write. Often they consider their own experience to be extremely limited and uninteresting, definitely not the stuff of which Writing with a capital W is made. So the teacher needs to devise a strategy for combating this view. The best writing at 'A' level seems to me to be that which does originate in deeply felt experience. Consequently I try and get students to see their own experience as a valuable resource for all kinds of writing. One way I have found to do this is to use oral story-telling as a starting-point. Students, working in pairs, tell 'stories' based on significant moments in their past. The teacher then asks the students to change partners and retell the stories to the new listener, perhaps this time rethinking where the story should begin and what the most effective opening sentence might be. Several versions might be tried out before the students move on to a new partner. This time they may be asked to concentrate on bringing more dialogue effectively into the story or, another time, on finding the best point to end the story. Gradually the narrative is shaped as the students move around the group. When the teacher feels the moment is right, he or she can stop the story-telling and ask the students to draft a written version, fast, to a time limit. The hope is that this will provide a rough first draft which can be taken away and worked on later. This activity also provides an opportunity to explore the relationship between oral and written narratives. There are many other games which can make writers aware of the potential lying within their own experience – for example, giving a 'voice' to different parts of oneself can be a way into dramatic monologue, or drama, or narrative voice in fiction, and it also provides an opportunity for self-discovery, a way to find out what 'voices' are available to the writer.

Finally the kind of hobbies, interests and passions students have developed often provide rich material for persuasive, instructional and informative writing, as long as they can take on the challenge of addressing a specific audience. Here again students, in my experience, often take such interests for granted and need to be made aware of the expertise that they have available to them.

The writing games, then, will serve a number of purposes: making students aware of different strategies, keeping them writing regularly with specific limited objectives, giving them some idea about where to start looking for subject matter and developing their capacity for 'creative recognition'. However there is still a big leap to make into taking responsibility for a longer piece of work. At this point it is an advantage to share a model of the processes involved in writing with the students. Garth Boomer proposes a fascinating model in his *Fair Dinkum Teaching and Learning*, which provides a convenient starting-point if one is required.[9] The National Writing Project also suggested a number of models.[10] However the best model is one that is worked out (in diagrammatic form perhaps) with the students starting from, and being continually tested against, their own experience of writing. (If the student is studying language this can be combined with a study of the behaviour of young children when writing and by talking to them about what happens in their head when they write; if she is on a literature course she might research the observations about the actual experience of writing made by professional writers.) The purpose of a model is partly to provide a common reference point for student and tutor when discussing problems in the student's attempts at longer pieces of course work. It can help to identify the area of difficulty and provide a focus for discussion. It may be that the student knows what she wants to do but is having difficulty in organizing and structuring the work, or that the purpose is too vague and there is consequently too much material which is irrelevant. A clear idea of the processes involved in writing will help the student become more conscious of the choices which she is making at different points in the writing and this goes some way towards reaching the goal mentioned earlier of developing the writer's capacity for self-awareness and self-criticism. A starting-point might be a collective list of mental activities which occur between deciding to write and finishing a piece. What questions do we ask ourselves when we write? Again it is also extremely beneficial if the tutor writes herself so that any comments she makes about writing are solidly based on personal experience. I am not suggesting here that any credence should be given to the kind of model that proposes a mechanical step-by-step progression of the 'brain-storm' – plan – draft – edit – polish up variety. Any model would have to allow for the recursive nature of composing activities and avoid the implication that a piece of writing exists in some way completed in the mind before it is written down. In fact many students do possess a model of writing which is something like this (which may account for the panic which some of them feel when faced with a blank piece of paper). Discussion of a variety of models of writing, the consideration of statements by professional writers and, best of all, a visit by a 'real' writer, will help them begin to see the potential of writing as a means of discovery.

The JMB English Language syllabus requires that the student's awareness of the writing process is made explicit in the form of a commentary on the original writing. Although this is not an obligatory or examinable element in other courses at 'A' level I still feel that it is a valuable learning tool in its own right. Not only does it force the writer to consider carefully the way the piece was put together and what elements went into it but it also enables the apprentice writer to evaluate his own work. Instead of the students feeling that they are expected to produce perfection and anything short of that must be considered a failure, writing a commentary can help them assess their own work realistically in terms of what they can expect of themselves at this stage in their writing development. In the commentary they can talk about what they have achieved and what they have failed to achieve. A good commentary will be based on the kind of thorough understanding of the writing process mentioned in the previous paragraph. That is, it should be based on close observation of what actually happens when we write, elucidating conscious choices and yet acknowledging that the unconscious may also have been involved. The JMB examiners' report states that the commentary should be 'written as though for an audience of fellow writers rather than for examiners'.[11]

A commentary encourages the writer to see the work as a stage in his or her development as a writer and to reflect on what has been learned. It should be honest and exploratory. The worst commentaries invent a series of arbitrary 'conscious' choices and are works of fiction in themselves.

It seems certain that in future some form of 'original' or 'creative' writing will continue to be offered as part of some 'A' level syllabuses. It has been extremely popular with students. Teachers as well, in spite of the problems of assessment it can raise, seem committed to it. I remember a meeting during the early days of the 'A' level Literature 'Sheffield' syllabus (now syllabus C) where there was a proposal that the obligatory 'composition' element in the course work should be dropped because of the difficulty of assessing the work and because of the lack of any clear academic 'content'. The meeting discussed the issue for some time, focusing on the problems colleagues had encountered in teaching this part of the course. When the vote was taken I was surprised, given the largely negative comments that had been made, that it was unanimous in support of retaining the creative element. Since then there has been progress in devising effective, systematic methods of assessment. In the JMB Language syllabus, for example, the commentary and the obligation on the part of the candidate to state clearly the audience he is addressing and the primary purpose of the piece make assessment much more straightforward and less dependent on the literary taste of the assessor. Another reason why some form of creative writing is likely to continue to be offered at 'A' level, and indeed is likely to be expanded, is that it offers a logical continuation of work done at GCSE, especially in schemes where there is a large course work element. The original writing component of the JMB 'A' level Language is also very much in line with the view of writing which exists in the National Curriculum. I am thinking here of the emphasis on drafting and revising as well as the requirement to develop the ability to write in a range of registers for a variety of audiences. It is also likely that the movement towards modularization of 'A' levels will lead to more students opting for some creative writing element and that students will begin to take 'English' courses which combine elements of the existing language and literature syllabuses. This being the case many students will be taking a writing course at 'A' level which does not necessarily offer a privileged status to literary forms of writing. They could be coming out at the end of their 'A' level courses having practised writing radio documentaries, informative leaflets, political speeches and pamphlets on current issues, instructive writing of various forms including teaching materials, travel writing, manuals, newspaper and magazine articles as well as stories, poems and plays.

The fact that English teaching in this country has been based primarily on a study of literature has meant that where writing courses have developed it is literary forms which have largely been practised. The story, the poem, the play have dominated to the extent that the term 'creative writing' itself seems synonymous with literary writing. However developments in literary theory which question the extent to which 'literature' can be separated from other forms of discourse and developments in English teaching lower down in school, such as the National Curriculum and the GCSE with their emphasis on a variety of forms of writing, and Technical and Vocational Education Initiative (TVEI) which focuses on writing in the world of work, are all putting pressure on the privileged status of literary forms. Furthermore the kinds of teaching approaches I have mentioned, such as the workshop approach, do actually work extremely well for other forms of writing. At an adult writing group which I have attended for a number of years the assumption has always been that 'writing' means literary writing. However, on one occasion, an accomplished poet who had often read his poems to the group brought along a piece of political journalism he had written for a local paper. What struck me was the kind of feedback he received for this piece, which was primarily informative and persuasive, in contrast to the reaction he usually got to his poetry. The difference was that, where the comments on his poems tended to be tentative and subjective, even from highly literate and experienced members of the group, the comments on his article were far more direct. His aim was practical and specific: to alert a fairly sophisticated and committed readership to the possible long-term implications of certain recent events. The feedback was on the lines of 'your audience will already know that', 'that part sounds patronizing', 'the first paragraph doesn't command the reader's attention', 'what about changing the order here – it doesn't seem logical' and so on. He was able to take the article away and rework it thoroughly before submitting it (successfully) for publication. The point is that where the aims are specific, and the audience defined, it is much easier to say what needs to be improved and how it might be done. There are implications here for the kind of writing courses which are offered beyond 'A' level. It seems likely that as a result of experiences at 'A' level there will be a demand for a broader definition of creative writing than that offered by many institutions at present. This means that the question of the status of non-literary, non-fictional forms of discourse within creative writing courses will need to be addressed.

Notes

1 The Joint Matriculation Board Examination Council, *General Certificate of Education Regulations and Syllabuses 1991* (Manchester, Joint Matriculation Board, 1989) p. 39.
2 Ibid., p. 30.
3 The Associated Examination Board, *1993 Syllabuses. Advanced Level/Advanced Supplementary Examinations* (Guildford, The Associated Examination Board, 1991) p. 2.
4 University of London School Examination Board, *General Certificate of Education Regulations and Syllabuses June 1990–January 1991* (London, University of London, 1988) p. 258.
5 The Oxford and Cambridge Schools Examination Board, *Regulations for Certificate Examinations for the year 1991* (Oxford and Cambridge, Oxford and Cambridge Schools Examination Board, 1989) p. 351.
6 Quoted in Janet Emig, *The Web of Meaning, Essays on Writing, Teaching, Thinking and Learning* (New Jersey, Boynton/Cook, 1983) p. 48.
7 Seamus Heaney, *Preoccupations, Selected Prose 1968–1978* (London, Faber and Faber, 1980) p. 49.
8 Keith Johnstone, *Impro* (London, Methuen, 1981).
9 Garth Boomer, *Fair Dinkum Teaching and Learning, Reflections on Literacy and Power* (New Jersey, Boynton/Cook, 1985) p. 149.
10 The National Writing Project, *Writing and Learning* and *Perceptions of Writing* (Walton-on-Thames and Edinburgh, Thomas Nelson, 1990).
11 The Joint Matriculation Board Examinations Council, *GCSE Examiners' Reports 1987* (Manchester, Joint Matriculation Board, 1988) p. 13.

9

Teaching the craft of writing

Jane Rogers

Introduction

If creative writing is to be taught alongside academic subjects, and if part of the justification for teaching creative writing is to improve the critical skills of students of literature, then I believe it must be taught as a craft. By this I mean that students should be asked firstly to identify and consider the specific problems and tasks that a writer faces in constructing a story, poem, whatever. Secondly, that students should be encouraged to solve those problems for themselves by using several methods of which the most useful is raiding and copying from other writers. In this chapter I shall describe this process as it might be used for teaching prose fiction writing (that is, novel and short story). I have used variations of the ideas I describe with numerous students, most recently with BA undergraduates at Sheffield and Manchester polytechnics.

Before I launch into the detail of a proposed course, I should face up to those teachers of writing whose key word is 'inspiration', and who see their main task as helping students to 'self-expression'. I suspect they will not like my way of setting about a subject. Well, there is more than one way to skin a cat, as my granny used to say. Over years of working as a novelist, playwright and teacher of creative writing, I have become increasingly jaundiced with 'inspiration' and 'self-expression'. I am not denying that these things are important. I have taught workshops where it has been clear to me that self-expression *should* be the starting-point for the group: most specifically, groups of children who really wanted an opportunity to let their imaginations rip and first-time adult writers who lacked confidence in their ability to write anything and needed to be reminded of (or, sadly, to discover for the first time) the freedom and excitement creative writing can bring.

Students on exam courses in further and higher education are not in this situation. Whilst some of them may be enthusiastic poets or short-story writers, others will not be. What is offered to them as part of an academic course cannot be dependent upon their ability to be inspired and to express themselves. Are these things which can or should be examined? (Give Milton a mark out of 100 for *Paradise Lost*. How much of that is for inspiration? How much for self-expression? But is it *sincere*?) If, on the other hand, a student *is* interested in expressing him or herself, or is inspired to write a particular piece, well, that is a bonus, and something which any self-respecting teacher would go out of their way to encourage.

'Self-expression', 'creativity' and 'inspiration' in themselves are unhelpful concepts, for students and practising writers alike. They can induce imaginative paralysis ('I don't know what to write. I'm not inspired. I don't have anything I want to express...' which moves on depressingly swiftly to, 'I haven't got anything to say. I can't write.'). Or they can lead to the sort of self-indulgent sprawly mess with which all teachers of creative writing are familiar; the piece that sometimes calls itself a prose-poem, sometimes autobiographical fiction, and which deals at length with love and depression, thoughts of sex and death, poetic flashes from dreams, and deep psychological insights into the nastier aspects of humanity. What is generally most noticeable about such a piece is its lack of narrative structure or poetic form, the dearth of plot and characterization, the absence of humour and irony, the lack of narrative structure or poetic form, and the lack of intellectual rigour throughout. Such self-expression may be a beautiful thing, and can certainly have therapeutic value, but perhaps it should be confined to private diaries. It is inappropriate to encourage students to write such material as course work, and downright cruel to subject it to critical analysis by their fellow-students.

I find it worth reminding students, sometimes, that the inspiration or starting-point for a novel, for me, is a tiny thing in comparison to the finished product. It is a mood, or even a single image, or a half-grasped idea that I need to explore and properly understand. My hero, Orph, in *Separate Tracks*, sprang from a combination in my imagination of a very unhappy boy I once taught, and Stevie in *The Secret Agent*: the inspiration, if you like, was the mood generated by that character. That was what made me want to write the book. I held that mood, that flavour, in my head as I wrote, and tried to remain faithful to it, as I explored how the world treated Orph, and how Orph reacted. But remaining faithful to it was not inspiration. It did not cause the plot miraculously to take shape all on its own. In fact it made me work painfully slowly, because a lot of what I wrote was not relevant to that mood, or was not honest or accurate enough, and had to be jettisoned.

And even if you argue that the inspiration, since it is the starting-point, is the most important single part of the whole venture, well, it still cannot be taught. You can set up situations where you *hope* to inspire students, you can try to create the space for them to think and imagine, and you can strew interesting things in their way. But you cannot *make* a student have an insight or a mood or an image that they feel an obsessive need to explore and develop in a literary form. Which is probably just as well. What can be taught are techniques: the tricks and skills a writer uses. Not what to say but *how* it is said. And, of course, examining and understanding these techniques is an invaluable strand of literary criticism, which is itself the major part of most English courses at 'A' level and above. What better way is there of examining and understanding anything, than to try and do it yourself? How else do children learn? How else do we acquire all our spoken language?

Writing prose fiction: some techniques, ideas and examples

I have confined myself to prose since this is what I write, and I feel more at home with it. It is of course possible to teach poetry in exactly the same way, and I have done so in the past. (For anyone planning such a course, I would recommend Paul Fussell's splendid *Poetic Meter and Poetic Form*, which is stuffed with examples, and gives a thorough and accessible analysis of the effects created by different techniques in poetry. James Fenton's 'Poetry Masterclass' in *The Independent on Sunday* was also excellent; I would be surprised if his pieces were not published in book form soon.)

In all the exercises which follow I am assuming a basic workshop format to the class, so that, over a number of sessions, students will not only write their own piece on the subject set, but also exchange their work with other students, read, comment and constructively criticize each other's work, and (in those cases where they feel the work to be of sufficient interest and merit) rewrite and rework the original piece. In the course of discussing their work (either in pairs, in small groups, or in the whole class) students usually explain and defend what they have written, and show where they have found difficulty. All this, of course, helps to consolidate their skills both as critics and as writers.

1   Beginnings

Writers begin as readers. (Having made that bold assertion, I must admit that I am intrigued by Janet Burroway's suggestion that maybe they don't, any more; that maybe writing leads non-readers on to books.) Either way most people can tell a good beginning from a bad, by answering the simple questions, 'Would you read on? Why? Why not?'

I give students a selection of opening paragraphs, untitled, and ask them if they would read on. Any reasonably varied selection would do; I have used the following: Kafka, *Metamorphosis*; Carter, 'Company of Wolves'; Rushdie, *Midnight's Children*; Fay Weldon, *Little Sisters*; Toni Morrison, *Beloved* and Alice Walker, *The Color Purple*. Discussion of why/why not read on, will generally identify the following points, among others.

1 That you need something (a hook, an unanswered question, suspense) early on to encourage you to read further in a novel or story. Each of these openings raises that most fundamental and necessary question in the reader's mind: What is going to happen? To Samsa, now a gigantic insect? To the traveller through ferocious wolf-country? To Sallam Sinai, whose fate is linked with his country's? To the abused, innocent, pregnant 14-year-old? To Elisa the typist, visiting millionaires? To Sethe and her daughter, abandoned in the intolerably haunted house?

2 That style can attract or repel, and this may come down to individual taste as much as anything else (some loving Carter's detailed descriptiveness, some finding it clogged and difficult).

3 That immediacy is highly effective (a specific image or sensory impression: Samsa's bed quilt which is about to slip off, Morrison's kettleful of chickpeas smoking in a heap on the floor).

4 That pace is vital. Who hooks us quickest? Which is the best opening sentence? I think it is Kafka's. Not only is there the instant banner headline hook – man turns into insect – but also the expectations he raises with 'uneasy dreams', which tells us that Samsa's day-to-day life is troubled. Questions about fantasy and reality are raised: were the uneasy dreams real? Was he *really* an insect, or was that 'only' a dream? What does his being an insect mean? The writer is promising us something which is going to work not just on the level of 'what happens next?', but also on the level of ideas. The image conjured is precise – Samsa in his bed, transformed into a gigantic insect. The trappings of ordinary life, the bed, are not left behind and even the fantastic transformation has a realistic aspect, in that the man's body size is relatively unchanged – the insect is as big as the man was.

   With any luck, others in the group will prefer other openings, and argue for them.

5 That one generally feels the need of human interest fairly swiftly. The one to discuss in this context is Carter; four paragraphs in, we still have no hero or heroine. Does it matter?

6 That, as well as all this, a reader expects to get a sense of what the whole book or story is going to be about.

I then ask the students to write their own beginning to a story; it is not necessary for them to plan the story or know how it will develop or end. The task is simply to write an opening page which will grab a reader and make her or him want to read on.

Aims of the exercise

1 Introduction of suspense and understanding that it does not have to be a great clanging 'Whodunnit?', but that suspense can also be generated by a character, by a place, even an idea. The suspense may be anticipation of humour and entertainment to be generated by a writer's attitude to her characters (as in Weldon).
2 To be concise.
3 Consciousness of style; awareness of choices to be made. It is, incidentally, interesting that quite often students will choose to write an ending for this arbitrary beginning.

2   Plotting

There are no new plots; they have all been used before. Shakespeare was recycling them 400 years ago. Certain plots have proved enduringly popular, both with writers and readers. What are they? And why are they so successful?

1 The outsider or stranger (in a different village, city, country, class, sex, culture, planet, time): for example, *Shane, Gulliver's Travels, Room at the Top, Jane Eyre*, most of Henry James, *The Fifth Child, The Scarlet Letter, The Enigma of Arrival, The Unbelonging, L'Etranger*.
2 Rags to riches: *Cinderella, Dick Whittington, David Copperfield, The Mayor of Casterbridge, Jane Eyre* again, etc. It is the single most used plot-line in popular fiction, one frequently used by Catherine Cookson, Jeffrey Archer and Helen Forrester.
3 Transformation (may be temporary or permanent, but the story interest centres on the protagonist's difference from his or her earlier state, and anxiety about how to get back, or excitement over strange powers or dangers inherent in the new state; or, quite simply, upon the theme that appearances can be deceptive). Examples: fairy stories (frog princes, hideous old women who are really beautiful young girls, wolves in sheep's clothing, etc.), *Alice in Wonderland, Honey I Shrunk the Kids, Dr Jekyll and Mr Hyde*, Kafka's *Metamorphosis, The Incredible Hulk*, horror stories about werewolves and vampires, novels about growing up, novels about dying, *Superman* and other superheroes. Of all the plot-lines I have identified with students, this one seems the real gem, giving rise to most interesting work. Maybe that is because it is open-ended – you might regain your original form, but you might not. You might be happier, but you might die. Maybe it is because our lives are a succession of metamorphoses anyway.
4 Disaster: Set up a difficult/disastrous situation, preferably with a limited number of characters, and see how they behave as things get worse. This is an all-time favourite film plot; characters are trapped in submarines, in sinking boats, in lifts, in aeroplanes that are going to crash, in burning buildings, in the path of hurricanes . . . Sometimes they are trapped with,

or at the mercy of, a lunatic, or murderer, or wild animal. It does not matter what the disaster is, it is just important to know that something very nasty is going to happen soon, and that is what generates the suspense. *Castaway* started with an apparently idyllic situation that then became disastrous. It is a plot-line that fairy tales often use, sometimes very amusingly. Grimm's story *The Boy Who Left Home to Learn Fear* shows a character enduring numerous terrors, willingly, and escaping from each cheerfully unscathed, simply because he does not react with the fear one would expect.

Suggestions of plots will vary wildly with each group of students; it will also be noticeable that many of the best and most basic plot-lines (such as thwarted love and good v. evil) are used simultaneously, or overlap. But, having identified a number of templates for good stories, students can then be asked to chose one and write their own story using that plot-line.

Aims of the exercise

1 Identifying the well used nature of most basic plots and being asked to do likewise helps remove that dreadful pressure to be original.

2 Plotting a story – giving it a decent shape – often seems to be the most difficult part of writing it. Working to a given plot and structure gives escape from that anxiety and a chance to concentrate on line-by-line writing. There is a satisfaction in this, comparable, I think, to the satisfaction Wordsworth suggests may be found in the sonnet's 'scanty plot of ground'. Sometimes it is more interesting and liberating to have the ground staked out for you, than to be given total freedom.

3 This is the best way I have found of making students aware of the great part a reader's expectations play in his or her understanding and enjoyment of a story. *Because* certain plots are well known – indeed, clichéd – it is possible to play upon the reader's assumptions about what will happen next. It is possible to upset those assumptions or manipulate them. Thus the plot can be used in reverse (riches to rags) or the hero can be given unheroic qualities of cowardice and ugliness; or the nasty thing in the woodshed can turn out to be harmless after all. What the reader is going to assume and expect about what happens next, at any stage in the story, is one of the factors a writer is bound to be aware of. It is insight into those expectations which frequently makes possible such diverse effects as irony, humour or heart-stopping shock. In the course of deliberately using a well thumbed plot a student has the opportunity to play with a reader's expectations.

4 Thoughts about how different writers use the same plots will arise, both from the initial discussion identifying plots and from group reading and discussion of the students' own stories. How many different ways can you tell the same story? From beginning to end, in chronological order. From end to beginning, in flashback. In the all-knowing third person. From the

hero's point of view. From the point of view of someone unimportant (cf. *Rosencrantz and Guildenstern are Dead*; it is a lovely device to use with any minor characters in great literature). From multiple conflicting viewpoints. From 400 years in the future, pieced uncertainly – maybe wrongly – together. And so on. Those simple choices of narrative voice and of sequencing of plot events make all the difference; and yet students often start (as readers and as writers) by not being particularly conscious that there is more than one way to tell the story.

3 Characterization

Here I think it is worth gathering together as many interesting and reasonably brief character descriptions as you can find; everyone will have their own favourites. Suggestions are: John Updike, *Rabbit Run*, opening paragraph of the book, p. 5; Doris Lessing, 'The Second Hut', *Winter in July*, p. 7, first two paragraphs; Raymond Carver, 'Blackbird Pie', p. 91, first two paragraphs; William Faulkner, *The Sound and the Fury*, first page; Jane Austen, *Pride and Prejudice*, pp. 1–2 (ending 'Mr Bingley might like you the best of the party.') and p. 3, the final paragraph of Chapter 1; and Charlotte Brontë, *Jane Eyre*, p. 140, bottom paragraph, to p. 141, end of third paragraph down.

After the students have read a selection, I ask them to pick out particular methods by which a writer can describe a character. This could result in a list roughly like this:

1 Through physical description – 'His wispy moustache hiding a strained, set mouth.'
2 Narrator's statement about character – 'She was a woman of mean understanding, little information, and uncertain temper.'
3 Through revelation of character's thoughts – 'He stands there thinking. The kids keep coming, they keep crowding you up.' Sustained use of a single character's point of view creates many interesting possibilities for the writer, including the notion of an unreliable narrator, as in 'Blackbird Pie'.
4 Through speech – 'My dear Mr Bennet, how can you be so tiresome? You must know that I am thinking of his marrying one of them.'
5 Through action – 'My sole relief was to walk along the corridor of the third story, backwards and forwards, safe in the silence and solitude of the spot . . .'
6 Through metaphor – 'Rabbit' Angstrom.
7 Through what other characters say or think about them – 'Listen at you, now,' Luster said. 'Ain't you something, thirty three years old, going on that way.'
8 By association – with a place, mood, occupation (Carruthers was a soldier; Angstrom a basketball player; Benjy in Faulkner's piece wanders near the golfcourse because they shout 'Caddie', and it is his beloved sister's name.)

Building up this list could lead on to discussion of which methods in particular students feel to be most effective. Physical description is interesting to examine in detail because of the truism that readers visualize their favourite characters for themselves ('the man in the film didn't look anything like he did in the book'). How much physical detail do you need to trigger that imagining? One carefully chosen feature can do it. Lessing's sentence about Major Carruthers's smile 'which was too quick, like the smile of a deaf person afraid of showing incomprehension' works so well, both as physical description and psychological insight, that I would argue she could lose a lot of the surrounding description.

I opened my second novel, *Her Living Image*, with a long paragraph of physical description of the heroine, which I would now cut completely. I had reasons for it: I wanted the novel to begin four-square and traditional, with a portrait of the heroine, to lull the reader into a sense of security and familiar territory – because I then disrupt that completely, fracture the heroine's life and present two alternative versions of her story. But, whilst I still think that that impulse was, artistically, quite a good one, I now feel irritated by the slow detail of all that physical description at the beginning and would be prepared to sacrifice my artistic intentions for the sake of a more pacy opening – I would open straight into paragraph two.

I would draw attention to the difference between the Brontë and the Austen, as illustrations of what the first and third person can do. Brontë has immediacy and passion, and swiftly generates our sympathy; Austen has distance, irony, humour. I have taken two extracts from Austen because of her masterly mixture of dialogue which demonstrates the characters' attitudes (especially Mr Bennet's irritation and boredom with his silly wife) and then her incisive authorial summary. Each method complements the other, and although in the second passage we are being told what to think, we feel little inclination to disagree, since the married couple have revealed themselves through their dialogue. Austen's summary focuses what we have already observed.

Faulkner's first person is, in his author's word, an idiot; and Carver's is certainly unreliable ('I lost it, or else misplaced it.'). Lessing and Updike make an interesting comparison since both use physical detail as a major element in revealing character, although Updike brings us much closer in than Lessing does, by showing us how Rabbit thinks.

Having read and criticized the passages, I would ask the students to describe a character in any way, or combination of ways, they chose. Most writers admit that their characters are taken wholly, or in part, from real life, and I would suggest that students do the same.

Aims of the exercise

1 To be aware of the variety of ways in which a reader can be given information about a character, and to gain some experience of using a number of these methods.

2 To see that it is often more effective writing to show than to state: that is, to dramatize a character, to show him or her through speech and action, rather than through a summary of his or her qualities. But following on from that, to be aware of when and why a writer might choose to summarize rather than to dramatize – for the sake of conciseness (in this batch, Lessing and Carver's are the openings of short stories, the rest novels) or maybe to give clear notice of the narrator's attitude to the character (Austen).

3 To attempt at least a short piece in the first person, from a fictional character's point of view, in order to experience the range of possibilities this opens up for the writer, most especially in the area of what information be given or deliberately withheld from the reader. It can be a very useful exercise to describe the same situation – say an argument – from two different characters' points of view.

4 Setting

As with characterization, I would fling a heap of examples at students, such as: Graham Greene, *The Power and the Glory*, opening paragraph; Graham Swift, *Waterland*, page 2, paragraph 3 ('We lived in a lock keeper's cottage' to the end of the following paragraph); Charles Dickens, *Hard Times*, pp. 65–6; and Jayne Anne Philips, *Black Tickets*, p. 261, final paragraph, to see what they are like and why. The power of settings to create and reinforce mood are clear from these, especially the Greene and Phillips. It is also possible to see how a writer can use the physical detail of a setting to illustrate and expand upon themes and arguments of a novel (Dickens and Swift). I would ask students to name novels or stories they have read which have memorable settings. How does the setting feed into the mood/tone/ themes of a piece of writing, when it is working well? How much setting can a reader stand? Can you have too much of a good thing? It is difficult to extract from Hardy, but he is a writer whose books should be discussed in this context. The short story 'The Yellow Wallpaper' by Charlotte Perkins Gilman could also be read for discussion, since the setting here is symbolic (of the frustrations and mental imprisonment of a whole class of women at a specific time in history). This writing exercise is one of the most simple; write a description of a place which seeks to evoke a particular mood for the reader. It's the sort of exercise a painter might try, with landscape. Students can exchange their work and get direct feedback on what, in terms of mood and emotion, their pieces have suggested to readers.

Aims of the exercise

1 To see setting as yet another element over which the writer has choice, and through which she or he can manipulate the reader's attitude. Again expectations can be fulfilled or foiled; the thunderstorm could be the background to a joyful reunion, or to a hideous row.

2 Inevitably the issue of style will arise because it is so linked in with mood; and questions like 'how many consecutive adjectives can a reader bear?' will have to be faced up to. Many readers (including myself on occasion) skip descriptions which they know to be of great literary merit, because they want to get on with the story. This is something which would-be writers need at the very least to talk about!

5 Dialogue

Passages to look at might include: Alice Munro, *The Beggar Maid*, pp. 103–4; D.H. Lawrence, *Sons and Lovers*, pp. 260–61; Ursula Le Guin, *Orsinian Tales*, 'Conversations at Night', p. 34 and Ernest Hemingway, 'The Killers'. Ask students to note what effect writers are achieving through dialogue which they cannot get through straight description. The answers will be in the area of immediacy, drama, economy, accuracy of mood. In the passages from Lawrence and Munro in particular, the movement and development of mood, and quicksilver emotional changes, are registered economically in speech and yet would be cumbersome – maybe impossible – to describe in a report or summary of the dialogue. Lawrence gives us an equal insight into each character's pain; Munro captures that mercurial movement towards understanding, a shared sense of humour. All have dramatic power; they are showing us people, not stating things about them. We hear, and are left the space to make up our own minds about, the characters. In the Le Guin, the setting is evoked economically in the cracks between the dialogue. Hemingway uses repetition to create menace and a sense of brutality-in-waiting.

Ask students to write a prose incident using mainly dialogue.

Aims of the exercise

1 To see that writing good dialogue is not the same as writing lifelike dialogue. (If this is not clear, ask students to tape an improvised – or real – conversation, then transcribe it. It will almost certainly make tedious reading.)
2 To see how effective the combination of narrative prose and telling dialogue can be, and to become aware of the rhythms generated by each; really, this is about understanding pace.
3 To see that dialogue can often be much more economical than narrative description.

6 Style

This will have been covered to some degree by the exercises, but that is no reason for not doing it again. Look at a number of passages which are as varied in style as possible; for example: James Joyce, *Ulysses*, p. 665; Barry

Hines, *Kes*, opening page; Sue Townsend, *Adrian Mole*, pp. 44–5, 'Wed. March 11' and 'Thur. March 12'; Russell Hoban; *Ridley Walker*, opening two paragraphs; Virginia Woolf, *To the Lighthouse*, pp. 168–9 (from 'But with Mr Ramsay bearing down on her . . .'; and Laurence Sterne, *Tristram Shandy*, opening page. Talk about which are easy to read, what are the advantages and disadvantages of stream-of-consciousness, of cinematic realism, of a narrative voice limited by age or vocabulary and so on. Ask students to write a description of an everyday event (such as taking the dog for a walk, bathing the baby) in the style of one of the above. If you have time, try it in the style of more than one.

Aims of the exercise

1 People are often surprised by how easy it is to mimic a style. If you *can* mimic it successfully, you have immediately got a much better insight into how it works.
2 For some students the copy will move quite naturally into parody, which is fun, and opens up yet another way of telling a story. Exercises so far have been a little short on humour!
3 No one is suggesting it is useful for students to write cod Hemingway for the rest of their lives, but finding a voice of your own is to do with picking and choosing amongst other voices, trying things out, seeing what effects can be achieved with different styles. It is perfectly acceptable for painters to learn by copying techniques, and no less so for writers.

How can you express yourself if you lack a range of interesting techniques with which to do it? Encourage students to be pretentious, to be ambitious, to copy the best writers. Above all, advise them to copy what takes their fancy. Most writers do it automatically, subconsciously; and know it. Most have to stop reading other people while working on their own stuff, because it is so easy to fall into someone else's style.

Note: The suggestions made here should not in any way be seen as a list of rules and prescriptions for writing. One of the most marvellous things about writing is that there are no rules and that anyone, with basic education, from 6 to 106 years, can do it. No way is more correct than any other; as ordinary a thing as a sentence can in Dickens's hands be a single ominous word – 'Fog' – and in Faulkner's an immensely complex analysis lasting for pages. The whole point, for a would-be writer, of exploring these different ideas, is to become more aware of the wealth of possibilities available: to try on styles and techniques like hats, and see what they do for you. And to better understand, thereby, what they do for other writers.

References

Austen, Jane (1960). *Pride and Prejudice*. London, Heinemann.
Brontë, Charlotte (1973). *Jane Eyre*. London, Penguin English Library.

Carter, Angela (1984). *The Bloody Chamber.* London, Penguin.
Carver, Raymond (1989). *Elephant and Other Stories.* Collins Harvill.
Dickens, Charles (1974). *Hard Times.* London, English Penguin Library.
Faulkner, William (1979). *The Sound and the Fury.* London, Penguin Modern Classics.
Greene, Grahame (1970). *The Power and the Glory.* London, Heinemann Educational Books.
Hemingway, Ernest (1974). 'The Killers' in *Men Without Women.* London, Penguin.
Hines, Barry (1975). *Kes.* London, Penguin.
Hoban, Russell (1983). *Ridley Walker.* London, Picador.
Joyce, James (1969). *Ulysses.* London, Penguin Modern Classics.
Kafka, Franz (1968). *Metamorphosis and Other Stories.* London, Penguin Modern Classics.
Lawrence, D.H. (1966). *Sons and Lovers.* London, Penguin.
Le Guin, Ursula (1978). *Orsinian Tales.* London, Panther.
Lessing, Doris (1984). *Winter in July.* London, Panther.
Morrison, Toni (1988). *Beloved.* London, Picador.
Munro, Alice (1987). *The Beggar Maid.* London, King Penguin.
Phillips, Jayne Anne (1984). *Black Tickets.* London, King Penguin.
Rogers, Jane (1990). *Separate Tracks.* London, Faber and Faber.
Rogers, Jane (1990). *Her Living Image.* London, Faber and Faber.
Rushdie, Salman (1982). *Midnight's Children.* London, Picador.
Sterne, Laurence (1970). *The Life and Opinions of Tristram Shandy.* London, Penguin English Library.
Swift, Graham (1984). *Waterland.* London, Picador.
Townsend, Sue (1985). *The Secret Diary of Adrian Mole.* London, Methuen.
Updike, John (1984). *Rabbit Run.* London, Penguin.
Walker, Alice (1986). *The Color Purple.* London, Women's Press.
Weldon, Fay (1980). *Little Sisters.* Sevenoaks, Coronet.
Woolf, Virginia (1969). *To the Lighthouse.* London, Penguin Modern Classics.

10

Makings from models:
Story-telling and story-writing

Joan Michelson

'Close your eyes. What do you see? What are you thinking? Words? Colours? Shapes? Textures? The spoken repeating? What is passing before you in your private darkness? Write for five minutes without stopping.' This is a useful exercise for most, if not all of us. It aids focus and concentration and provides us with content as a starting-point.

In one of my sessions, a primary school child wrote, 'Flowing, rushing, the egg timer never stopping. On and on goes mum. The house is being run by her.' In another, a secondary school child wrote, 'To be the best./Mash down the rest./Let my pen's ink flow./When I'll stop I don't know./Thinking of new ideas,/of my new career./Hoping for a brand new poem./The words are now flowing.' A polytechnic student: 'Tired from running up the stairs. Why are we doing this? Hands are cold. Will friends look up at me at the disco?' A member of a workshop for adults: 'The heaped laundry ready for packing on a clear bright day. Lambs marked with red. And the terrible boy won't get out of bed.'

I have approached the writing of this chapter so many times, made so many admirable but discarded starts, that I am ready to close my eyes. Suppose I too find my way through mind-flow. In *The Craft of Fiction* (1921), Percy Lubbock refers to the 'shadowy and fantasmal form of a book . . . It melts and shifts in the memory.' Writing workshops share these characteristics. However meticulously we have prepared ourselves and however many exercises we have up our sleeve, or in our notebooks, the workshop sessions melt and shift.

Yet it is these that I propose to report on, recalling and recording process in two sample sessions. The first is a three-hour block from a 14-week module taken by second- and third-year Humanities degree students at Wolverhampton Polytechnic. The second is the morning session, or the first half of a day school offered to adults as part of the City University Centre for Continuing Education. Both focus on aspects of story-making, especially, but not exclusively, creating and controlling plot; and both take their bearings from models: the first, a short story by the Latin American writer, Jorge Luis Borges (1976), the second a Near Eastern tale from *Elijah's Violin and Other Jewish Fairy Tales* (1983), selected and retold by Howard Schwartz. Although the make up of the two groups differs and the objectives of the first include story-*writing* while that of the second is story-*telling*, there are more similarities than differences. Indeed the London-based professionals who attended the story-telling workshop proved to have similar habits of approaches to literature to the polytechnic students. Both groups could have been served by attending each other's sessions. And work from either could be used as a contribution to continuing course work or for a one-off endeavour.

While there are distinctions to be made between story-*writing* from models and story-*telling* from models, the issues addressed have much in common. As story-writing proceeds from telling, or talking through parts of the narrative, there is significant overlapping. Therefore the following points are relevant to both. It is no secret that loss of story-telling is a cultural impoverishment and that the experience of telling and enhancing our tellings with language has long been displaced by media offerings. Moreover those drawn to stories who find their way into our workshops as part of higher or continuing education have already adjusted to a critic's approach. The educated reader responds with an analytic, abstract, impersonal and often passive vocabulary. In this sense he is cut off from the essential emotional centre, given body by the sensual enticements of orchestrated concrete language. His attention directed elsewhere, he fails to see how the work is constructed. Moral and philosophical interpretations of stories, ideas derived from stories, and cultural commentary abound, frequently to the obscuring or even exclusion of basic story urges and components.

The workshops described below address these habits through approaching available stories anew. Also, as vehicles for release, the workshops help people to let go and to take risks with and within narrative. En route they facilitate exercises in essential craft skills. The workshop differs from taught literature courses in setting its target beyond the mastery of a body of knowledge to the ability to create a new body: for example, a story.

Telling before writing is a particularly effective way of beginning. As language is lifted off the page and placed in space it is brought into relief. The literary shows itself to be just that, while the spoken, natural and immediate, finds itself advancing into its rightful place. Energy of action displaces the more relaxed and distanced rhythms of reflection. Drama and character are created, taking ideas into the mouths of created character and giving rise not only to the development of character but also to the dramatic interaction of differing ideas.

Telling is used as an aid in the first session. In the second it becomes the primary mode. Telling serves because of its insistence on spoken language, gestures and significant actions. Telling clarifies basic story components and lines of development with an economy which puts discussion into the shade. Once we have told the story we have a speaking voice to write with and an improved ear for the language of our characters. In the writing which follows the tendency to employ the learned language of the essay is averted. In sum, these workshops serve to release students from habits of intellectual approach by bringing stories to life and by probing the ways writers and tellers have used to accomplish this.

A story-writing workshop

The model selected for the session was a story by Jorge Luis Borges, 'The Intruder', from the collection titled, *Doctor Brodie's Report* (1976). We began the session by reading a comment from the Afterword. 'The Intruder' haunted Borges for 30 years before he set it down. He started with the idea of two brothers who loved the same woman. To safeguard their friendship, the woman had to be sacrificed. He thought of setting the story in California but talked himself out of it because he did not know the place well enough. ('My knowledge of California was merely bookish.') In the end, he set it in his native city, Buenos Aires. We went over this paragraph for useful advice. Students made notes, then spoke out:

1 Use settings you know well. Avoid those you do not.
2 One way to start a story is with a basic plot-line.
3 In your plotting, you might discover a problem which has to be resolved. Borges has to determine what happens when two brothers love the same woman. He decided that they sacrifice the woman. Why? Because they value their friendship more.
4 One way to view the plot is in terms of problem solving. You ask yourself: What happens when? What happens if? And then what happens afterwards?
5 There is a beginning, a middle and an end. You have to decide what to begin with, what happens in the middle, and where to end.

Borges purported to end with the sacrifice. How did he describe it? We turned back to the story. Someone contributed that he did not exactly describe it. Cristian tells Eduardo that he has killed Juliana and so they had better get busy before the buzzards take over. The story ends just before they bury her, with the brothers embracing. The last sentence emphasizes the relationship between the brothers.

'And where does Borges begin his story?', I asked next. The answer to this was so problematic we put it aside to deal with later in the session. In the meantime, we made a list of questions that arise from the story. How do the brothers sacrifice the woman? Does the woman prefer one of the brothers to the other? Do the brothers confide in one another? If not, how do they know about each other's relationship? Does one go first and the other follow? Is there a moment when one finds out about the other? How does he react? What happens then? Do they make other (different) decisions before they decide to sacrifice the woman? If so, what are these decisions?

We reread the story for the progress of its plot and then retold it in a few sentences. One student said,'There are two brothers. They don't communicate. They do communicate with this woman. They try to live without her but can't. They banish her but secretly go to see her. When they find out they have been doing the same thing, they take her back. When this doesn't work, they kill her.' Another student said, 'It's the tale of two brothers who have a steadfast relationship. Jealousy interferes. The only way out is to kill the woman.' And a third student, 'Two brothers fall in love with the same woman. They share her for a while. Then one of them kills her. Together they bury her and keep their bond.'

Next we retold the story using some of Borges's details – whorehouse, piebald, hitching post and so on – and calling his characters by their proper names. This was one of the retellings: 'Cristian brought Juliana to live with his brother Eduardo and himself and then Eduardo fell in love with her too. One night Cristian went out, telling Eduardo to use her if he wanted to. So for a while they shared her. Then one afternoon they had a discussion and resolved to place her in a whorehouse. After that, secretly, each started visiting her at the whorehouse until one day Cristian came upon Eduardo's piebald at the hitching post. So they brought Juliana back home. One Sunday Cristian killed her and buried the body under some hides heaped on his oxcart. He told Eduardo to help him bury her. The brothers embraced.'

Letting this telling stand, we scanned the story, each seeking ten words that we could use for our own stories. As lists were produced we saw movement in different directions. Some led towards particulars depicting the time, the place and the situation. Others were thematic: love, shared, cheating, for example. And there were mixtures of the concrete and the conceptual: brothers, ties, women, enmity, money, forgetting, Cain, possessing, arguing, heat.

We selected four words from the pool: 'ties', 'enmity', 'partnership' and 'being trapped', and tried an exercise. Working in groups of four, the students shaped their own plots from these words. They had 20 minutes for the task. These were the plots they produced:

1 A happy unmarried couple have a child. Then they get married. Enmity sets in.

2 A father forces his daughter into an unhappy marriage. He is rich and his will stipulates that, if they divorce, she will inherit nothing. The couple stay together although, unknown to them, her father changes his will.
3 Business partners dislike one another. A letter arrives announcing that one has won a prestigious business deal. Over drinks the winner confesses to embezzlement while his partner confides that he is having an affair with the winner's wife. They dissolve their business and agree to forget the secrets they have shared.
4 Childhood friends become business partners. They share their lives until Geoff gets a girlfriend. Tom longs for Geoff's girlfriend. She is young and dynamic and everything Tom wanted to be. The relationship between the men is in jeopardy.

We reviewed these plots. There was a question about endings. Do you leave them open or closed? Borges completed his telling with a killing but he could have chosen to leave the story open-ended. Or could he? Perhaps a better question is: if he had, how would this have altered his telling? The question of narrative stance arose. Before turning to it, especially since it was tied in with the opening of the story, we pushed our plotting one stage further. We changed the people into animals. The animals could be real or imaginary. The plot came quickly and spontaneously from the group.

One student began, 'There were two cats. One stole the other's food. Tibbles and Tabby. Tibbles stole Tabby's piece of fish.' Another student picked up the story. 'Tibbles had Tabby's piece of fish. Tabby had lost his fish. They had a fight. The owner was blind.' And another. 'No, the owner was away. It doesn't matter whether he was blind. A neighbour was in charge of the cats. One ate all the food. The other had to scavenge. One grew fat and slow; the other grew lean and wild. The fish was a magic fish, a frog in disguise.' And others. 'A whale in disguise. A prince of a whale. When Tibbles ate the fish, he swelled to the size of a whale. From inside his belly, a voice spoke: "Get away you lot." And the man from the circus came to carry mega-cat off so he would be shown in all the corners of the universe. And he was beamed by satellite. But as he came on to the screen, the whale spouted and all that could be seen was a fall of water.' (Have Cain and Abel, transformed by Borges, produced Jonah in the belly of the Whale dissolving into foam?)

Pleased with this and relaxed by the whimsy of our group construction, we returned to the Borges story for further observations and analysis. Now we considered the narrator. As mentioned earlier, Borges tells us that the story haunted him for 30 years before he set it down. In the story he uses a first-person narrator who refers to himself as a writer and appears only in the opening paragraph.

We reread the opening paragraph:

People say (but this is unlikely) that the story was first told by Eduardo, the younger of the Nilsons, at the wake of his elder brother Cristian, who died in his sleep some time back in the nineties out in the district of Moron. The fact is that someone got it from someone else during the course of that drawn-out and now dim night, between one sip of mate and the next, and told it to Santiago Dabove, from whom I heard it. Years later, in Turdera, where the story had taken place, I heard it again. The second and more elaborate version closely followed the one Santiago told, with the usually minor variations and discrepancies. I set down the story now because I see in it, if I'm not mistaken, a brief and tragic mirror of the character of those hard-bitten men living on the edge of Buenos Aires before the turn of the century. I hope to do this in a straightforward way, but I see in advance that I shall give in to the writer's temptation of emphasising or adding certain details.

What do we know about the narrator? He is setting down a story he has heard, twice, in different versions years apart. Why does he inform us? It is a preparation for his variation. He argues that, although the story is old and known, and he hopes to tell it in a straightforward way, he will change it to suit his vision. As if laying all his cards on the table, he describes his view of the events he is about to unfold: 'a brief and tragic mirror of the character of those hard-bitten men living on the edge of Buenos Aires'. He goes on to locate his story in time: 'before the turn of the century'.

Now it is useful to have some dates. When was Borges born? The frontispiece gives us this information: 1899. When did he write 'The Intruder'? In our search we turned from the copyright dates of the collection, to the acknowledgement page, to the Bibliographical Note at the back. 'La intrusa' (The Intruder) was first published in an edition of 52 copies illustrated by Emilio Centurion and privately printed by the Buenos Aires bibliophile Gustabo Fillo Day in April 1966. We recalled that Borges said he was haunted by the story for 30 years before he set it down. If we could take this as a fact, although it might be fiction, we felt we could assume it was a story he heard as a young man and that, by the time he heard it, it was already a generation old. By the time he wrote it, at least 50 years stood between him and the event.

We reviewed: (1) the material Borges started with was a told tale, possibly a tall tale, passed from one generation to the next; (2) he teases us with its veracity: 'People say,' he begins, '(but this is unlikely)'; (3) besides telling us the tale itself, he tells us a brief tale of the tale. The narrator claims to have heard the story from Santiago Dabove, who claims to have heard it from someone who got it from someone else late in the night after the wake of the elder brother, Cristian. On that night, while the men were sipping mate, Eduardo, the younger brother, clearly distraught and perhaps not in his right mind, having lost the person he was closest to, told the story. Being told in the small hours and on such an occasion, the story acquires a ghostly, haunting quality; it is also made suspect. The first version was told to the narrator in another town. Years later, while he was in Turdera where the story had taken place, the narrator heard the story again. The time between the tellings is eclipsed. At the same time, the time expands into the continuous time of once upon a time.

Why has Borges gone to such length to introduce his story? (1) He has established his freedom to invent; (2) he has extended the ending by including the death of the older brother; (3) he has moved the story forward in time, by giving it rebirth or rebirths, and distanced it for us; (4) he has shown us some of the tricks of story-telling, encouraging us to see and take pleasure in the interplay of fact and fiction.

At this point we recalled the plots we had sketched during the earlier part of the session. Suppose we distanced them in time and retold them as reported stories. Suppose for instance that the business partners who had confided their sins in one another – the first embezzlement, the second adultery with his partner's wife – were long dead. Suppose too only one person had inherited their secrets. This was the illegitimate son born of the adulterous liaison. Let us call him Duncan. It is Duncan's story, but Duncan is not the narrator. Suppose Duncan has been dead for some time. People talk. Tales travel. The narrator, who is going to be the writer of the story, is an outsider. It could be any of us. What is the objective of the telling? A mirror to the character of the times and the circumstance? Duncan's moral dilemma? Confession and aftermath?

Or suppose we think about the granddaughter of the woman forced to remain in an unhappy marriage because she feared her father would dispossess her? The granddaughter, Mrs Christine Bok, has died in a distant land. What might be known about the characters? What might we leave mysterious?

The cat story, too, part parody, part tall tale, could be distanced and differently told. What happened to the generations that mega-cat produced? Did he found a new race? Or was he an exception, an aberration, a social outcast? Did he inhabit a separate world? Did he have exceptional know-ledge? Must it be a 'he'? If time had permitted, we would have written paragraphs about mega-cat and read them out. The session, however, was over. If anyone was motivated to pursue any of the starts we had made, I would be delighted and we would hear them at the next meeting.

To conclude, this analysis of Borges's tale helped us to locate and open up story-writing territory. In particular, the distancing devices he employed prompted us to relocate conventional and melodramatic events within the resonating form of the tale. Beyond that we were alerted to a number of aspects of the craft, including the importance of plot and the design of the story.

This is not all we could have done with this five-page gem of concision. We could have looked at the way Borges introduces his characters; placement of images, especially that of the worn Bible, the only book in the house, 'the roaming chronicle of the Nilsens' which yokes the tale he is telling with the telling of the tale; inclusion of material that precedes the time of the events; incorporation of habitual behaviour. We might have observed that the first two-fifths of the story prepare us for the tale and that understatement, the off-staging of violent episodes and reportage contribute to his concision. And more.

A story-telling workshop

We began the session with a telling. I raised a withered, gilded palm leaf and let it drop to the floor. 'The Golden Feather', I said. I laid a large tortoise-shell comb beside my golden feather, added a white crocheted serviette, a visored cloth cap and a long fringed scarf. There lay the story, not the bones exactly, nor the actions, but the props I needed to make my way from the beginning to the end.

The feather was my first find. It had two functions. It led me into trouble and was my magic-making helper. The comb was my other helper: when I combed my horse, he began to talk and to advise me. The serviette was my stage curtain and the handkerchief in which I wrapped whatever the king had ordered me to bring to him. The cap, turned one way or another, was the uniform issued as I rose through the hierarchy of the king's guard. As for the scarf, worn belt-like around my waist and then loose from my shoulders, it marked the transformation of the horse into a wise old man.

I went on to tell the story in a version too long for inclusion here. I followed the traditional sequence of three set tasks for the hero to fulfil in order to win the hand of the king's daughter. Raising and lowering my golden feather, I reached the garden where stood the tricky doubles, the Tree of Life and the Tree of Death, only one of which was mirrored in the reflecting surface of my feather. I climbed the Tree of Life, netted the golden bird, picked the golden apple and won the golden girl. All this came to pass because of my horse, who was a wise man under a witch's spell. After I made my third journey, he took a bite of the apple and was suddenly himself proposing to carry me skyward on the winged fringes of his rabbinical scarf. As we flew, we came upon the castle where the golden apple's fragrance inspired the caged bird to such singing as melted the hearts of men. 'Guard of 100 and 1,000, you will marry my daughter this very night!' the king commanded. And that very night the wedding celebrations began.

My story was a revised telling of Howard Schwartz's tale which was a written retelling in English of a Greek tale from the oral tradition. I was attracted to the story by the central image, the golden feather, and those which followed it: cage, bird, song. With these as guides, I had a way in to the plot and could begin my telling.

'The Golden Feather' is relatively straightforward. Roaming about with his horse, a lad sees a golden feather. His horse warns him to leave it on the grass but the gold glitters so brightly that the lad cannot resist. Not knowing what to do with the feather, he decides to give it to the king. The horse carries him to the king and the lad encounters hierarchies of power. Rewarded, challenged and threatened, he sets off to perform three set tasks. First he must capture the bird, then he must bring back the golden cage, thirdly he must find a way to make the bird sing, each of these within three days or he will lose his head. With help from his wise and empowered horse, the lad succeeds. And as he does so, the wise man is released from the spell which turned him into a horse. Not long after the lad marries the princess, the king dies. And the wise man lives in the castle as the king's minister for many happy years.

I altered some aspects of the Schwartz version and made numerous changes in my way of telling the story. I reported and analysed these for the students. For instance, because I could not integrate it, I left out the opening in which the lad's father, a merchant, gives a fine specimen of a horse to each of the lad's eleven brothers and an ugly colt to him. In my telling, for the sake of economy, I eliminated repeated descriptions. Also I left out the rabbi's explanatory story, which occurs at the end. I felt it sufficient for him to bite the apple and be transformed. Also, since no other details made the story specifically Jewish, I did not name him 'rabbi'. I wanted to allow him to come from Jewish culture or another, giving the story a wider application. Further, I did not want to add the complexity of his need to return three times when his motivation for the journeys appeared to be helping the lad. If his helping masks more personal aims, the story raises questions about the wise man's character. After all, he advised the lad not to pick up the feather. Yet, because he disobeyed, the two of them had to return to the garden and go through the actions for breaking the spell. If the breaking of the spell was on the horse/wise man's mind, would he have done nothing to have helped himself? For instance, he could have kept silent when the lad reached for the first golden feather. This aspect of the story appears to embody a conflict I could see no way of resolving. If the wise man had colluded with his own fate by failing to warn the lad, how would the story have carried its moral lesson?

But need the story carry it? Suppose the lad picked up the feather without being told anything. The horse might be waiting, watching, secretly hoping. The story might direct itself to his transformation by means of the travels of the golden feather. If so, would it help the listener to know the rules by which the spell might be broken? And would that information need to come at the beginning? A retelling might explore this. The story might be told from the point of view of the horse. (I said this to the group.) 'Quite a tall order,' a woman responded. 'Or from the point of view of the princess', suggested a different woman. 'Why should she get married? Could she be a feminist?' 'It's your choice.' 'How much liberty can you take with the story?' 'As much as you want to take. Think of it as a launching pad to take off from. The objective is to honour story-telling, not this particular story or particular version of the story.'

'The gold touch was from King Midas', a woman said. 'The bird reminded me of Hans Christian Andersen's "Nightingale",' another said. 'Yes', I said, 'I reread the Hans Christian Andersen before I started working on my telling. I thought about releasing the golden bird from the cage or having him fly out. How would the story be altered? In the "Nightingale" the natural creature is contrasted with the mechanical which breaks down. The true beauty of music is created by a singer who is free. But in "The Golden Feather", before he can be overpowered by this aesthetic truth, while he is shivering in response to it, the lad captures the bird. He values his life more than the beauty he has found. There might be another story waiting on the uppermost branch if, because of the music, the lad does not capture the bird.' 'The story doesn't have to be believable, does it?' someone checked. 'It can have magic in it but has to be credible within the premises you set up.' I gave a final instruction: 'Make notes if you wish but prepare to tell your story without looking at them. If you are stuck, your notes are there for reference.'

In the story told from the point of view of the princess, the princess takes on the manoeuvring and plotting of the jealous guards. Because she did not want to marry the lad, she told her father to send him off for the bird, the cage and the song. At the same time she worked very hard to make herself ugly, 'fat and spotty', so that if, unfortunately, he did accomplish the set tasks, he would reject her as, at first, he had rejected the horse. We spotted a possible problem here. We wondered if he might not have learned from his experience with the horse that ugliness can be changed. The princess was also given mobility. In the source version, and my own, the world of court never travels beyond its walls. The recreated princess, however, sneaks out first to the stables where she overhears the horse talking to the lad and she rides after them, fast enough to cross the forest, enter the garden, rush past the twin trees and reach the gold dust pit where there is a golden palace which is more splendid than any in the world, before they do. This time the palace is filled with the fragrance of the apple and it is she who wants to eat the fruit. The bite transforms her into a dazzling beauty. The lad falls at her feet. She tells him she has no intention of marrying anyone. She wants to do things. She does not know what they are yet, but she will find out for herself.

The story told from the point of view of the horse revised the opening section I had left out of my telling. The student began, 'There was once a wise man who always had his head in a book. Whenever the weather permitted, he took his books into the fields to read in the sun. In the last of the summer sunshine he was sitting under an apple tree. Around him were some of the fallen fruit. Just as he closed his hands around an apple, an angry man on a horse appeared. "Eating my horse's apples, you thief." In the next minute he had turned the wise man into an ugly colt and dragged him off to market. Now, in the market place on that day, was a wealthy merchant in need of a horse. He was wealthy, that is, but by that time of day, he had spent all his money except one gold piece. "What can you offer for one gold piece?" he asked the horseman. "Well you can have that miserable specimen if you like." The exchange was made and the merchant delivered his purchase to his youngest son. When the lad saw his horse, he looked so disappointed the horse burst into tears on his behalf. Then he spoke: "Can you get that comb from behind my right ear?"

After this point, the story-teller lost her daring and returned to the version I had told. This resulted in a loss of her emphasis on the wise man and his problem. After hearing each member's version, we returned to my telling as a source version and reworked scenes in a variety of ways: for example, without having a narrator or without using words. We looked back at some scenes. The lad never seeks out the horse merely to chat. The king has always set him a task impossible to perform without the help of his horse. While seeking help, the lad grooms and feeds his animal. (So there is a reciprocal giving.) The horse, meanwhile, is mapping out the course of action.

This is as much as time permitted and certainly it is enough to illustrate some ways of working with spoken narrative. In response to this particular workshop, a student wrote that she had been helped to 'come out from behind the barricade of the thesaurus, dictionary and polished prose' and that, since participating in the workshop, she had become 'aware of untold stories buzzing around us like ghosts desperate for mouths to slip out of'. Also, having experienced a day school, she was going to look around for a course.

And what do I say in conclusion? Like Percy Lubbock, I have 'tried to disengage . . . various elements of the craft . . . and this has involved much rude simplification of matters that are by no means simple'. The author is a craftsman. The critic looks at the author's work to see how it is made. In the writing or story-telling workshop, we weave a course between these two. And we go further, tricking our imagination into play.

References

Borges, Jorge Luis (1976). 'The Intruder' in *Doctor Brodie's Report*. London, Penguin.
Lubbock, Percy (1921). *The Craft of Fiction*. London, Jonathan Cape.
Schwartz, Howard (1983). 'The Golden Feather' in *Elijah's Violin and Other Jewish Fairy Tales*. London, Harper and Row.

11

Methodizing:
Drama and creative writing

Michael Mangan

Those RULES of old discover'd, not devis'd,
Are Nature still, but Nature methodiz'd.
(Alexander Pope, 'An Essay on Criticism')

In this chapter I intend to discuss two distinct ways in which the techniques of drama relate to the context of the creative writing class. Firstly, there is the issue of workshop games and exercises. These are in common currency in acting schools and on practically based drama courses; since their aim is primarily to stimulate the creative imagination, it is worth while exploring how these may be of use to the creative writing group. I shall be concentrating on the topic of generating narratives, and it should be stressed that these narratives are not necessarily theatrical ones; the first part of this chapter concerns the teaching of any kind of fictional narrative, not merely the teaching of play-writing. This is dealt with more specifically in the second part of the article, since play-writing is a field of creative writing teaching with its own specific agenda. In discussing both of these areas, however, I shall be looking at the notion of creative freedom and artistic restrictions.

Improvisation: language-based games and exercises

To look first, then, at the field of workshop games and exercises.[1] An actor's training involves, among other things, a certain amount of work in improvisation. The aim of this work is to facilitate a variety of skills, including concentration, the ability to interact with others, the ability to develop themes, characters and situations and so on. The keynote of improvisation work is exploration. The point is not to reach a particular goal, but to take things wherever they want to go. This may – indeed it usually does – involve a certain degree of 'nonsense' work, which can take place on a number of levels, from tightly structured improvisation games through to completely free improvisation. In this chapter I shall be concentrating primarily on the more structured manifestations of improvisatory work, since it is in these early stages that I believe the more general applications for teachers and students of creative writing lie. In particular I would argue that the 'spirit of improvisation' which these games aim to encourage and develop is one which is relevant to the teaching of creative writing.

To take an example of a highly structured improvisation game, we might look at one which is particularly well used by drama teachers and which has also started to find its way into creative writing classes: the 'Word-at-a-Time Story'.[2] In this game the rules are simple: the group sits in a circle and they tell a story round the circle, keeping strict sequence but with each person contributing only one word at a time. Thus a person starts with one word, the person on his left adds another word, the person on her left adds another word and so it continues. Such a story might go: 'I ... went ... down ... the ... street ... and ... I ... saw ... a ... green ... chimney ... on ... the ... pavement ... and ... it ... exploded ...' – and so on.

Some of the benefits of this game to the creative writer as well as to the trainee actor should be obvious. There are, it is true, some skills which this game will develop which an actor will use more directly as part of her craft than will a writer: the element of interpersonal response which the game generates, for example. It could be argued that, precisely *because* writing is so often a lonely, isolated, even antisocial activity, this group-dynamic aspect of this game has a compensatory value for the writer. There are also benefits, however, which will be recognized as more immediately relevant to the development of writing skills.

Primarily the game opens up certain areas of imaginative territory. Almost always the game becomes silly. Bizarre events, impossible collocations, ridiculous juxtapositions are the norm. The logic which pertains is the logic of the absurd – or of the subconscious. The surreal happenings and landscapes of the stories which emerge often prompt the remark that they are 'dreamlike', and the impression which players often get is that they are beginning to explore – or to create – a group 'subconscious'. Yet no member of that group needs to feel that she is about to be psychoanalysed, that it is *her* subconscious which is on parade: the whole group shares responsibility for what the narrative throws out. Whatever happens belongs to everybody in the circle. The game offers a safe way of exploring areas of language and areas of the imagination where it seems that there are no rules except the rules of syntax.

This element of shared creativity also offers the players (initially) a way out of one of the major 'binds' of the creative writing class – the need to be impressive, that self-conscious striving after originality which is often a

major block to any true creativity. Improvisation teachers are fond of in-
stancing as a paradigm for their art the master juggler, whose first task is
to teach his student how *not* to catch the ball; how to let it fall to the ground
naturally rather than straining after it, how to simply empty her hand and
receive the ball rather than trying to make things happen.[3] The lesson is
that of going with the flow, of accepting what happens and working with it
rather than imposing the will on it. Telling a story by using only one word
at a time commits the individual player to *not* having total control of the
narrative, to accepting and making use of the structures which the group
presents to him. Occasionally a player will express a frustration with the
limitation of only being able to contribute the single word, or he will try
to contribute more: this is usually an indication of a need to control the
direction of the narrative and betrays an anxiety about simply accepting
'whatever happens'. A central feature of improvisation, however, lies not in
control but in the flexibility of response to the vagaries of the developing
situation – however absurd, disturbing or even mundane they may turn out
to be. As Keith Johnstone puts it,

> I ask the students to set themselves up in such a way that they'll learn
> as quickly as possible. I'm teaching spontaneity and therefore I tell them
> that they mustn't try to control the future, or to 'win'; and that they're
> to have an empty head and just watch . . . It's this decision not to try
> and control the future which allows the students to be spontaneous.[4]

In the hands of some teachers, this touch of Zen may perhaps become a
little disingenuous. Nonetheless its value is evident: the first and most difficult
task is to free the imagination.

And yet freeing the imagination also involves putting restrictions upon it.
I have described this game as a highly structured one, and so, in many
respects, it is. People take turns in a strict order, and are allowed only one
word at a time. It is within this rigid structure that the free play of improvisation takes place, for one of the paradoxes of improvisation – and of
creative writing as well – is that creative freedom often arises from formal
restriction. Yet, so as not to betray the improvisatory spirit itself, the game's
own structure should also be subject to improvisation. The game in fact
works best when it is played not once but many times, with time for discussion
and feedback between 'rounds'. In this way the game itself will become,
almost inevitably, a developing entity, as different groups evolve different
rules to deal with some of the issues which this game throws up. For example, how does the group want to deal with punctuation? As should be
obvious, without any punctuation at all the whole thing will ramble inde-
terminately, or at best degenerate into an endless series of 'and' clauses. So,
the students having played the game a few times with this as a problem, a
rule can be introduced concerning whether 'full stop' counts as a word in
itself, or whether it is something to tack onto a word already said. In the
above example, then, it might be the person who said the word 'exploded'

who decides that this is the end of the sentence, or it may be the player who follows her.

More fundamental is the question of adverbs and adjectives. Players quickly catch on to the fact that these are useful ways of avoiding a decision, as in: 'I . . . went . . . down . . . the . . . street . . . and . . . I . . . saw . . . a . . . green . . . striped . . . ugly . . . horrible . . . great . . . big . . .' etcetera. If the group is reminded that the point of the game is to develop a story, it will usually realize quite quickly that the deferring of a decision through this kind of proliferation of adjectives prevents the narrative from advancing. It may be happy with this or – more usually – it may decide that no adverbs or adjectives are allowed, or that no two can go together, or whatever answers the needs of that particular group. Rules developed by groups I have worked with have included:

No adjectives or adverbs.
No adjectives, but adverbs permitted singly.
No elephants.[5]
Each word to begin with a subsequent letter of the alphabet.
The game to be played at a certain speed.
The story to include certain key words.
The story to end with a particular word or phrase.
The story to incorporate simultaneous actions.
The story to be a serious one.
The story to be written down rather than spoken, and passed around.[6]

Ideally these rules develop in relation to the group's own sense of the story-telling which they are involved in: each group can devise its own rules as it gets more familiar with the principles of the game and wishes to explore its possibilities. In this way the rules operate as responses to a growing sensitivity to narrative technique. From this comes the perception that rules can be creative rather than merely restrictive: not being 'allowed' to churn out endless adjectives forces the mind to look for more creative solutions.

Thus, while the game's initial value is that of getting narrative ideas and images flowing freely, as it develops it begins to raise questions concerning narrative craftsmanship. In this respect it has things to offer which are more directly relevant to the student of creative writing than to the improvisation student. One of these derives from precisely that instinct to control (or at least predict) the future against which Keith Johnstone warns the improviser. It is almost impossible to sit in a group which is telling a word-at-a-time story and not attempt to anticipate future developments of the narrative, to guess where the story is going to go and start preparing your own contribution accordingly. Successful improvisation demands a suppression of the desire to determine completely the shape and direction of the story, so that the improviser learns to wait for his own turn and simply respond to what is there at that particular moment. For the creative writer, however, it is also instructive to pay attention to precisely those mental anticipations in order to focus on a particular aspect of narrative art. For the word-at-a-time story provides an experiential workshop in what Stanley Fish has called 'affective stylistics'.[7] By slowing down and randomizing the narrative, the game illustrates the way in which a listener is continually predicting the outcome of a story, then modifying those predictions, then making new predictions based upon the modifications. It offers a demonstration of the way in which, for the reader or listener, narrative is primarily an experience which unfolds through time. A sentence starts and, as it develops, there develops along with it an implied dialogue between it and a listener. For example:

> The ... (what?) man ... (what about him?) got ... out ... (his gun?) of ... (gaol? bed? doing the dishes?) the ... bath ... (aha! and?) and ... put ... (on his trousers?) away ... (oh) the ... (what?) pelican ... (eh?) which ... was ... licking ... (his knee?) its ... (my turn!) lips ... Full stop.

As the infinity of possible stories collapse into the one actual story, the audience's imaginative interaction with the narrative takes a particular shape. The creative writer of any genre who understands that she will be leading a reader through a series of questions, expectations and predictions is already well equipped. It is in connection with this lesson that the proliferation of rules about punctuation, adverbs, adjectives and so on take on their meaning. By playing the game of the word-at-a-time story the student is engaging with one of the essential dimensions of imaginative writing – the temporal.

I have spent a long time talking about this one rather elementary game because it seems to me to encapsulate many of the principles of the theatre improvisation workshop which are of use in the teaching of creative writing. The improviser's 'empty-hand' attitude, the tendency to explore rather than create, the openness to the bizarre and the unusual, the relationship between formal structure and creative freedom – all of these seem to be attributes as important for the writer as for the dramatic improviser.

There are other verbal games of improvisation which offer possibilities for the creative writing group: several of them, like the word-at-a-time story, encourage the release of ideas through shared responsibility. Some of them are familiar from other disciplines, such as the simple game of word association. Others are specifically concerned with ways of structuring narrative: for example, there is 'Fortunately ... Unfortunately ...', whereby the story is told a sentence at a time, with each sentence beginning either with the word 'Fortunately' or with 'Unfortunately'. Thus:

> Fortunately I managed to catch my train ... Unfortunately it was in an accident and derailed ... Fortunately I had nearly reached my destination at the time so I decided to walk the rest of the way ... Unfortunately it was pouring with rain ... Fortunately a man in a car gave me a lift ... Unfortunately he was a homicidal maniac ...

This exercise usually generates a narrative which proceeds to shape itself in terms of a sequence of obstacles which are then overcome – a technique which can easily be related to the larger structures of story-telling.

A more difficult game is suggested by Ronald James and Peter Williams; they call it 'Exploring a statement'. With the class sitting in pairs:

> One partner starts with a phrase, the other partner adds a phrase which helps explore the given situation, and as the dialogue proceeds the exploration gets wider and deeper. Questions are not accepted as contributions since this puts a responsibility on the partner away from the speaker. Similarly, phrases which merely agree with what has been said are not acceptable since these do not further the exploration . . .

An example of such an exploration might be:

> 1) Fred was upset when it fell in the pond
> 2) He'd only filled it in the night before
> 1) His missus had been on to him for years
> 2) She'd always wanted ducks
> 1) Got it from her father
> 2) He had his in plaster on the wall
> 1) The family never had taste
> 2) Came of living in a lighthouse . . . and so on[8]

This game, when played well, tends to produce a narrative which initially explores backwards in time from a given point, throwing up a series of incomplete details which then need to be given a structure which relates them to one another.

Improvisation games of this sort have the effect of introducing participants to the mechanics of narrative from the inside, as it were. Stories get told come what may, and students get a chance simultaneously to participate in and observe the telling of them. As well as releasing certain image-clusters, or allowing the exploration of material which might otherwise be labelled as 'unacceptable', or 'trivial' and thus suppressed, the games inevitably throw up questions about structuring narratives – questions which students can later relate to their own individual work.

For what might appear to be obvious reasons, I have concentrated on specifically verbal improvisations in this discussion of the kinds of theatre games which might be of use to the creative writing class. Nonetheless it should be added, albeit in passing, that there are many physical and non-verbal improvisation techniques which can be used with equal success in the generating and discovering of narratives. Wordless story-telling, through use of mime, mask, gesture and caricature is fertile ground for the writer. As for the verbal games, however, there are many variations on the ones which are mentioned here and interested readers are directed to works by theatre practitioners such as Johnstone, Barker, James and Williams, and Hodgson and Richards.[9] Verbal improvisation is a learnable skill with a few basic principles which, once mastered, allow access to many areas of imaginative spontaneity. These games and exercises, initially done in pairs or groups, give way to individual work once some of the basic principles have been grasped.

A play-writing workshop

If one axis of the teaching of creative writing relates to the 'freeing of the imagination', another is concerned with craftsmanship. Most experienced writers understand the principle exemplified by the word-at-a-time story: that the demands of craftsmanship are not necessarily restrictions but can themselves be liberating. Many beginning students, however, find it simply oppressive to discover that there might be such things as principles of craftsmanship in play-writing, and insulting to be told that they should take cognizance of them. And creative writing teachers may well respond ambivalently to such a protest; nobody, after all, wants to turn out students who can do little more than paint by numbers. What needs to be stressed is that the 'rules' of craftsmanship are actually facilitating techniques, rather than a series of commandments. Analogies concerning sportsmen or musicians are trite but telling: learn the basics and how to operate within them – then, after that, you can break the rules creatively.

Nonetheless so-called 'rules of craftsmanship' mean very little in the abstract. There are some play-writing manuals, it is true, which offer summaries of such rules:

> The essential factor for arousing interest: conflict . . . The conflict formula: M + G + O = C. Main character(s) + Goal + Opposition = Conflict.

> Main characters must be clearly defined, capable of holding audience's sympathetic attention.

> Goal must be credible and interesting.

> Opposition must be strong: 'a play is as strong as its villain'.[10]

Some students find these kind of formulae comforting. Most find them nebulous. What is important, then, is that the student find out about craftsmanship for himself. Much of this finding out can only be done through the practice of playwriting itself, but some short-cuts are available, and their function is not so much to 'save time' (writers *need* to waste time getting things wrong) as to encourage at an early stage – before the necessity arises to defend one's own writing from criticism – the notion that mistakes are possible in play-writing, and that they are usually best avoided. The following exercise is concerned with the notion of discovering some basics of playwriting craftsmanship through working out how *not* to do it.

The extract below is one that I wrote for a seminar group at the University of Sheffield in order to point up some basic dramaturgical errors. In using it in class, it can be presented 'cold', as an exercise in critical analysis or – more honestly, for few students enjoy having tricks played on them – it can be explained that it is a piece of deliberately bad writing. In either event it is explained that what follows is supposed to be the opening few minutes of a full-length naturalistic play called *Rag Doll*, which details the breakdown of the relationship between a mother (Elaine) and daughter (Ruth).

Rag Doll

Characters
ELAINE – mid-fifties.
RUTH – her daughter, twenty-seven.
ALAN – her ex-husband, sixty.
EILEEN – her other daughter, twenty-one.

The action takes place in Ruth and Elaine's home. The time is the present.

Act One

The living room of a shabby-genteel middle-class house. One or two pieces of 'good' furniture, including a Louis Quinze sofa, over which, however, a pot of red paint has been spilled. The paint is still wet.

In one corner a TV is on with the volume turned up high, showing *Cagney and Lacey*.

ELAINE enters. She is in her mid-fifties, and wearing fashionable clothes. She carries a British Airways shoulder bag. She looks around, expecting to see somebody.

ELAINE: [calling] Ruth! Ruth, darling. Mummy's home. I'm back from America. The plane got in early from New York and I only had this one bag to bring through customs and I got a taxi really quickly so I'm back.

RUTH comes in.

RUTH: Mummy! Mummy, darling. You're home.

They hug each other.

RUTH: How was America?

ELAINE: America was lovely.

RUTH: Did you bring me anything back?

ELAINE: I certainly did, you young minx, but you'll have to wait until I've unpacked before you see what it is.

RUTH: Oh, go on, tell me now!

ELAINE: No – but it is something special.

RUTH: Go on.

ELAINE: No, you'll have to wait. Oh all right, then – it's a tartan skirt. (She begins to unpack.) And for Alan I bought this sweater, and for George these records. I got this picture for Katie, and these shoes for Beryl. And I thought Tony would like this plaster of paris bust.

RUTH: They're lovely. You are generous. What did you get Eileen?

ELAINE: Oh fuck! I forgot to get Eileen anything.

RUTH: Oh Mummy, she will be disappointed. She'll think you don't care. She's always felt that you loved me more than her, ever since we were children.

ELAINE: I know – but what could I do? I've always tried to treat you both equally, but she continually resents my treatment of her.

RUTH: It's not her fault either.

ELAINE: I know – but she doesn't make it easy.

RUTH: She felt really traumatized when you and Daddy split up. So many children of broken marriages believe that it's their fault when a marriage fails to work.

ELAINE: I know – but I have tried to reassure her about that. Daddy and I were simply incompatible.

RUTH: I know that but Eileen doesn't.

ELAINE: Oh no! What happened to the sofa?

RUTH: Oh. Yes. I was meaning to tell you about that, Mummy.

ELAINE: Is that red paint? On my favourite Louis Quinze sofa? You know how much I value that sofa. It was a present from Daddy when we were first married.

RUTH: You're always going on about that sofa.

ELAINE: How dare you!

RUTH: You're materialistic!

ELAINE: You selfish young woman! What happened? Were you painting something? Did the paint spill by accident? Tell me exactly what happened, Ruth. I only want to hear the truth.

RUTH: You care more about that lousy sofa than you do about me.

ELAINE: (shocked) Ruth!

RUTH: I hate you!

This is an exercise about mistakes of craftsmanship. Some readers might prefer to call them 'problems' of craftsmanship. They are mistakes (or problems) of different degrees – some arguable, some pretty absolute, some relating specifically to the opening of a play, others more general. They fall into various categories.

Errors relating to mode

One reader, coming across this passage for the first time, praised it as a piece of brilliant absurdist theatre in its own right – which would be all very well if it were not written as an essay in naturalism. It is certainly true that much theatre of the domestic absurd reads like bad naturalism; it is also true that for some people even competent naturalistic writing seems so heavy-handed as to be almost self-satirizing. However the point is – without getting too sophisticated about things – that good naturalism is, in any case, much harder to write than most people suppose. *Rag Doll* is about the difficulties of writing in this rather conventionally naturalistic style, but similar exercises can be constructed for Brechtian, documentary, agit-prop, avant-garde and other kinds of theatre writing, since all of these can be done badly, too.

All of the mistakes which are included in the extract are ones which I have seen in attempts at serious naturalism carried out by inexperienced writers. The point needs to be stressed: a writer should know what effect she is aiming for and should have the skill to bring about that effect. For some writers, *any* effect which their lines have on the audience is sufficient; they are happy enough if a line which is written as a soul-searching comment elicits a hearty guffaw from the audience who hear it as irony. Such writers rarely have anything to say that is worth hearing in the first place.

Errors relating to dramatic language

There are significant differences in writing for the page and for the stage. A greater awareness of the sonic values of language is vital, as is an awareness of the way an audience will both hear and mishear. For example, the names of main characters in this piece are Elaine, Alan, Eileen – all perfectly plausible in themselves, but poor choices since in an audience's mind they will be too easily confused when spoken.

Repetition is a great tool for the playwright, but it can be misused. On the page Elaine's continual repetition of the formula 'I know – but', which takes place between lines 24 and 32 does not look too bad. Spoken, it sounds terrible. Moreover, it is echoed in Ruth's reply in line 34: 'I know that but Eileen doesn't', which is slightly different in structure but which has been preceded by so many 'I knows' that an audience will inevitably hear it as part of the same pattern. A similar problem arises out of the exchange between Elaine and Ruth in lines 35 and 36, where Elaine's 'Oh no!' elicits Ruth's response of 'Oh. Yes.' Repetition does not have to be direct to be ineffective.

Register seems to be a particular problem in this extract. Presumably there are still 50-year-old mothers today who might call their daughter 'you young minx'? There are certainly 50-year-old mothers who say 'Oh fuck!' Just possibly there are 50-year-old mothers who would use both of these phrases within seconds of each other. But is the writer aware of the resonances set up by the juxtaposition of these two? Or of the sudden shift of Ruth's language into textbook psychology as she defends Eileen? Students who have a good training in analytical disciplines – literary criticism, for example – might well argue plausibly at this point that there could be good reason for the apparent disparity between the registers; perhaps, it might be said, it shows the violence beneath the apparently loving surface. Certainly these kinds of changes of register *can* be used to good dramatic effect; more often they occur as they do in this exercise – as moments which will convince an audience only that the writer has not 'found a voice' for the characters. This leads us back into the debate about the mode in which the writer is working: what might work in one mode will not work in another.

Rhythms are also something which students might want to consider. Ruth's line 'You're materialistic', for example: what is it about it that makes it sound so flatfooted? And, conversely, what happens when the following lines (44–5) are spoken out loud; 'Tell me exactly what happened, Ruth. I only want to hear the truth.'?

Errors relating to staging

The need for playwrights to be continually aware that their ideas will have to be given material form by directors, designers and actors cannot be overstressed. Different writers respond to this need in different ways. Many give only the most minimal staging directions, leaving as much as possible up to the director and designer. Others, thinking in terms of stage images, provide a great deal of information which is integral to the play. There are no rights and wrongs concerning this: however it is sensible for any writer who *does* want to provide a lot of stage directions to ensure that he has thought them through fully. For example, if a British Airways shoulder bag is all Elaine is carrying, can she really produce all those gifts from it (lines 15 ff.)? And how necessary are all the gifts anyway? (See comments under 'Control of information'.)

Then there is the red paint ('still wet'!) on the Louis Quinze sofa. Possibly this is a brilliant symbolic effect, relating to blood, materialism, violence and menstruation. On the other hand it may be an expensive waste of a good piece of furniture. Will it be worth while in the end?

On another level, there is the kind of stage direction which seems puzzling in its triviality. In *Rag Doll*, the TV volume is on high at the beginning. This seems a reasonable idea – the set and the empty room suggest a certain kind of lifestyle. But how important is it that it should be *Cagney and Lacey*? Perhaps later developments will show – and perhaps they will not. But, in any case, the TV is then forgotten. Does the conversation therefore take place over it? Or does somebody turn it down? It may, quite properly, be asked whether it is the writer's problem at all or whether it should be up to the director to take care of issues like this. One answer to that question is that, if a writer starts specifying special effects, she should do so for a reason, and should be prepared to follow them through the scene.

Errors relating to control of information

One of the hardest basic jobs which a writer has to do is to perform that delicate balancing act between giving the audience enough hard facts for them to make sense of the events in front of them and simultaneously to allow the characters to speak believably. To inform without seeming to inform – that is the trick. In *Rag Doll* there are various attempts at this. There is Elaine's exposition to the empty stage as she walks in: perhaps a trifle flatfooted, repetitive and verbose? Expositions in general are particularly difficult, and perhaps this one is no worse than many real, staged plays. But what about the way in which information about the failed marriage is fed into the scene? Is this realistic? Artistically satisfactory?

Another simple decision relates simply to *how much* information to release at one time. Elaine lists the gifts she has brought for George, Katie, Tony and Beryl – none of whom (according to the dramatis personae) will ever appear in the play itself. At a time when the audience is being introduced to the various relationships which *do* exist within the play, is there any point in confusing things by introducing these 'phantom' characters?

Errors relating to structure

A common error of novice playwrights is to leap straight into the central issues, to throw everything at the audience in the first minutes of the play. Arguments are a particular hazard since the old cliché about conflict being the driving force of drama is true enough, and the argument is an easy dramatic device for getting things going on the stage. But the pacing of the conflict is crucial. In this play the argument between these two characters probably should not be at this point in the play at all, since the explosion in the first two minutes leaves the conflict nowhere to go for the next two hours. But, even if it is artistically necessary to start with a full-scale row, it can be paced better than this.

These are some of the main dramaturgical errors in this extract. There are others, but the reason for including this exercise is not to demonstrate exhaustively these mistakes but to suggest a process – a process of becoming aware of craftsmanship through a consideration of its absence. In a creative writing class which is concentrating specifically on play-writing I have found it a useful exercise in that students who are given it to analyse and criticize quickly begin to discuss, to discover and to debate what can and cannot be done on stage. They begin, as with the improvisation games, to formulate their own rules of dramaturgy. Often they are more zealous and prescriptive in their rule-making than I had originally foreseen: the paint-stained Louis Quinze sofa, for example, was something I had thought of as a rather dubious device. Often it is execrated as a total abhorrence, to the extent that I have been in the position of trying rather lamely to defend it ('Well, it *could* work, in some circumstances . . .'). However the point is not that an inviolable set of absolute rules should be arrived at, but that the issues relating to what constitutes good craftsmanship in a certain mode of writing should be explored.

An exercise such as this is only a beginning, although it can be re-introduced to a class with different examples at different stages and for different purposes. Screenwriting and writing for radio – both of which pose specific technical problems – can be discussed usefully in the context of a similar exercise. Nonetheless it is still a large step for a student to take from being able to criticize someone else's lack of skill to working skilfully herself. The aim of exercises such as these, however, is to point students towards a consideration of the craft of theatre writing, and to offer a way of discovering for themselves the kinds of rules, principles and techniques which will work best for them.

Notes

1 Some practitioners make a strict distinction between 'games' and 'exercises'. I do not, since I would argue that the only real difference between the two lies in the spirit in which they are approached.

2 Keith Johnstone, *Impro* (London, Faber and Faber, 1979) pp. 130–8; Ronald James and Peter Williams, *A Guide to Improvisation* (Banbury, Kemble Press, 1980) pp. 2–3.

3 Antony Frost and Ralph Yarrow, *Improvisation in Drama* (London, Macmillan, 1990) p. 2.

4 Keith Johnstone, *Impro* (London, Faber and Faber, 1979) p. 32.

5 It is extraordinary how frequently an elephant finds its way into these improvised stories.

6 Keith Johnstone talks of the ways in which the written exercise tends to develop in stages of seriousness, from the nonsensical through to the vulnerable. He includes an example of a sequence of word-at-a-time letters written by three of his students; the final one reads: 'Walls encircle me. My heart has walls which surround my blood, beating steadily and relentlessly it pushes through my veins because I am so alive. Talk to me please. The walls are thin and crumbling. Life is being drained from within my body. Stop the current. I must break through the walls which hold my body. Death will soon release the aching heart, but I am not afraid. Here is my heart, now take a piece and smash down my walls' (*Impro*, p. 136).

7 Stanley Fish, 'Literature in the reader: affective stylistics', *New Literary History*, (1970) ii 123–62.

8 Ronald James and Peter Williams, *A Guide to Improvisation* (Banbury, Kemble Press, 1980) p. 8.

9 Keith Johnstone, *Impro* (London, Faber and Faber, 1979); Clive Barker, *Theatre Games* (London, Methuen, 1977); Ronald James and Peter Williams, *A Guide to Improvisation* (Banbury, Kemble Press, 1980); John Hodgson and Ernest Richards, *Improvisation* (London, Methuen, 1966). See also Charles Marowitz, *The Act of Being* (London, Secker and Warburg, 1978); Antony Frost and Ralph Yarrow, *Improvisation in Drama* (London, Macmillan, 1990).

10 Raymond Hull, *How to Write a Play* (Writer's Digest Books, 1983) p. 76.

12

One month's work

— *David Craig* —

4 June

Jon (American, brought up in Belfast, father lives in Paris) has put in
a story for the Tuesday afternoon workshop which draws on the gamut of
his experience.[1] It's budded out from a guideline on 'Hunger' that I set last
month. He imagined a young American researcher in Paris acting on
Hemingway's tip in *A Moveable Feast*: to appreciate a Cézanne, starve for two
days before looking at the picture. Maddened by sensations (or the lack of
them), he calls on a connoisseur, perceives his hair as 'combed into lines
like record grooves', his tongue as 'Fresh liver rolling onto a chopping
board'. The three pages have grown to 17, the man has an Irish father: 'For
the first five years of my life he spoke only Irish to me . . . I have forgotten
all of it except for *Sinn Fein*, which means "ourselves alone", and *Pogue
Mahone*, which means "kiss my ass".' The prose is less level, more Modernist
than Jon's usual; it so wittily creates the whole personal culture of the
aesthete that nobody has much to say beyond a reading-out of favourite bits
with clucks of pleasure and sometimes a defining of the nuance. All I'd
marked as doubtful – ? delete – was a rather sententious paragraph starting
'When is it that you realise that your parents are just like other people?'

Also a story by Tracy (from Philadelphia), untitled – she has a thing
about titles and puts them off till 'later on'. A very attractive woman is
having her hair cut – to the roots. She wants to escape the slavery of being
a beautiful object (her partner's pet-name for her is 'Perfect'). The story's
strength is the extraordinarily physical evocation of being shorn, clipped

hair-ends 'like blown dandelion seeds on her cape', the 'new lightness taking her by surprise and reminding her of cartwheels'. All this is unimpeachable – a feminist fable – reminiscent (by chance) of Doris Lessing's *The Summer Before the Dark* where the soignée upper middle-class woman becomes 'invisible' after illness has aged her hair and face and she's dropped out to Brixton. For once, we discuss the social implications. Philip (veteran of many peace camps and thousands of hours of heavy-duty post-sixties discussions) is ready as usual to vet the subtext for possible cant. 'So the woman revolts against sex-object status – well, men get stereotyped like this too – men too can get sucked into living for their image . . .' 'Women much more so, surely,' Marian and Anne and Tracy insist, and Jon and I; the media drip with ads for cosmetics etc, directed almost exclusively at women. 'They get at men too,' Philip insists, they're persuaded they owe it to themselves and their virility to buy sleek cars.' 'That's not *themselves*', we argue back – women are programmed by restyle *themselves*.

7 June

Various cars take the whole gang of us to Clapdale, the university's very old leased farmhouse on the western slopes of Ingleborough, for a writing weekend, our second. Jon and Marian and Tracy and Philip and Graham and Anne (from Scotland) and three American undergraduates on a junior year abroad (JYA), Chris and Jim and Eric, and myself and Anne (my wife, Tutorial Fellow in CW). An atmosphere like fresh green honey swims through the dales, past limestone-jutting fellsides, brushing the heavy sycamore leafage, blueing distances. In mid-March, wintry moisture ran and blew in all directions and the raw chill was just gentled by stoking the iron stove to red-hot roaring-point with wet logs from the village next to ours, then dry reinforcements from Austwick down the road. Now the stove is almost for fun, a homely focus. Woodsmoke plus a great stack of spaghetti smothered in tomato paste and mince bring youth-hostel memories welling up. Here's the ultimate delight of teaching: concentrated days of brand-new writing, by an extended family of young (and middle-aged) talents, in surroundings like the best days of my youth . . .

8 June

Morning: delicious, tranquil stravaig with Anne along the skyline opposite. A mesh of limestone walls, shepherds' tracks, sheep-trods, criss-crossing a pasture so extended, and disappearing unfenced over the horizon, it has an American openness.

After that the mind-and-body are limbered to the acme of suppleness for the hours of writing. I suggest the guideline:[2] write an epitaph – read these aloud round the circle – pass yours to your neighbour on your right for her or him to develop a piece (prose or poetry; any form) based on the life the dead person might have had. I always invent the guideline; this time I'm borrowing one I worked to for Liz Cashdan at the Sheffield Verbal Arts Association conference on 27 April. It embodies a crucial idea: *any* material can grow in *any* direction. What you think of as 'yours' can mutate into a story/vision/myth which you hadn't (would never have?) dreamed of. (At Sheffield I wrote an epitaph for my mother's mother, a German lady with a 'von' in her name, who met her English husband, a teacher with a Cambridge degree, as he chaperoned a rich young man round Prussia c. 1890. He brought her to be a grammar school headmaster's wife in Aberdeen. My workshop neighbour, Spanish, metamorphosed my granny into a post-Second World War displaced person working in an English pub . . .)

The usual wealth of fictions and images starts to brew (though not in Chris from Minnesota, a highly conscious and close-grained person who dislikes the plunge and exposure of guideline work). Jon writes an extraordinary legend about the exodus of all dogs from an American city, heading north. How did he get this from the guideline? It doesn't matter. Anne: a naughty, vivacious, biting story about an MP's mistress. Jim from Oregan: a sad tale of a young poet sickening unto death. Eric: a rather abstract analysis of how a rigidly idealistic person becomes more open and free. I get his epitaph, for a woman who'd lived in the forest lands of New England, and turn it into a story about an old, happy, religious woman bottling fruit in the Canadian Maritimes, using an atmosphere I got to know travelling in Cape Breton Island and Nova Scotia for *On the Crofters' Trail.*

Wound up by four hours' writing and conversing, I embark on a chicken and mushroom risotto for eleven and accelerate so madly I can't pause to think of jobs for the people who come through to offer help. The cauldrons of food look right but they're *not savoury enough* – mass cooking needs an elephantine scale of provision, especially onions.

Later the writing still simmers. Eric tells me that the original of his epitaph was his Vermont grandmother. As he remembers the woodlands of his own recent youth, he warms to a reminiscence more vividly meaningful than anything he's written to date. He went camping in the woods with his brother. Both are night-blind. Their mother left them after dusk and got lost going back to her car – didn't like to go back for the torch because of her sons' night-blindness – stumbled through dense scrub and trees for two hours before winning through to the road.

9 June

Yesterday's blue and gold early morning dimmed whitely over, bleared into rain by 5 pm. Today's all gently dripping and shrouded. We leave tonight.

Let's use all the time. I suggest the guideline (two stages),[3] 'They do nothing. They are wrong. (At least a hundred years should pass.)' Stage 1 is meant to be practice in making eventlessness interesting. Stage 2 supplies the dialectical hinge, the crux, the mode of change, that seems to me right in guidelines (but almost anything works).

We've lived ourselves into the Clapdale atmosphere now; the chores (feeding the fire, refilling the geyser, washing up, coffeeing and nibbling and washing up, planning the next meal, washing up) have begun to do themselves. Creation is semi-continuous. People's eyes look past you, or unseeingly out of windows, focused on the next phrase, the next verse or incident; they wander through to kettle or sink with pad and pen in hand, come back through and at once write some more. Anne cunningly adapts the Member's Mistress's Tale to the new guideline and frames it all in re- miniscences over family photos imparted to the MP's great-granddaughter by her grandmother (Screaming Lord Such has become Prime Minister at the age of 82). Graham starts a serio-comic fable about how the Devil, at a loose end, crossed the yellow river on the day of the Feast of Unresolved Contradictions, when all the 'adult females' were 'preparing the traditional lumpen cake . . . a pie with the crust at the bottom'. Marian, the great worrier, says she'll work on things for the course that have been hanging fire (but this weekend could produce *more* fruits for the course!). Tracy crafts a story with cinematic recurrences of a slow-motion image: a china teacup is broken in a deep-South household, c. 1860 – the (black) maid is blamed by the young (white) lady who broke it – in the present, a gang of Caucasian roughnecks plan to frame a black man for a crime. Philip writes one of his hilarious time-warps: oak-worshippers at 'Abury' (Avebury) in Ancient Britain are pissed off because newfangled followers of the latest Moon cult have arrived to build a ritual site. (Crafty on Philip's part: this will slot into his novel, which skids about like Vonnegut from future to past to present.) I want to write about fatalism, credulity and it-can't-happen-to-us. The image of pale stones in a dried-up river-bed blinks into mind (because the rivers and becks in the limestone country of Craven so often dry up? But not *this* June). A ballad starts to form, cannily using assonances to avoid the rack of exact rhyming:

> Where the flood had been,
> Before their memory began,
> The river ran its channel
> Straight as the bole of a tree
> From the gorge to the coastal plain . . .

The five- or six- or seven-line verses are rough but they *happen* (I think); they're not unduly descriptive (my weakness).

After a feast of tuna-cheese-and-potato pie conjured up suddenly by Anne and Tracy, the fast workers, or those who feel cooped up behind the rainy window-panes, walk down the hill to see the show cave. In the common

room, and the kitchen and the dormitories, brains hum, pens speed –
people don't want to get off the log that's hurling them down river. Jim's
producing prose far better than the sentimental vagueness of his Dying
Poet. Graham scribes steadily, bearded lips twitching; once he says, 'This is
a minimalist piece,' mocking himself, pleased really. The semi-ballad rhythm
is working me, rousing me to the pleasurable maximum, I can *see* each next
necessary image or turn some minutes before it gets down onto the paper;
by 5 pm there are perhaps two verses still to come (the aftermath of the
flood, normality restored, where 'normal' equals the same old gullible human
nature carrying on much as usual).

We drive back to Lancaster through coolly steaming countryside. We're
so used to each other now: knowing what to expect from our various styles
– surprised, often, by new departures. Each session is another moment in
the nine-month conversation. The absence of strain is amazing and when
it does come (Marian's self-doubt, Philips's restless shoving of ever more
irons into his smouldering fire) it seems to be taken up into, put to use in,
more bouts of fruitful work. Or so I think.

Does this friendliness short-circuit criticism (which would not be true
friendship)? At Clapdale people seem to demur or judge adversely less than
at the university. After writing to a guideline, there's *always* less comment
on shortcomings – people still coming down from their own adrenalin high
can't readily switch to critical mode. A weakness of that method? Guideline
pieces, after revision, are often workshopped later, so criticism is still possible.

11 June

Before discussion of xeroxed pieces, I'm able to show the group a novel by
a predecessor – Kurt Tidmore, a hospital photographer from Denver who
came here to take the course in 1986 and is now a writer near Boston. He
wrote a novel for me by June; was dissatisfied and wrote another by hand-
ing-in date (September 1). Now his third (or fourth?) has been published
by Grove Weidenfeld of New York – *Bigger'n Dallas.* (The third by a member
of the course; the other two, Janni Howker's *The Nature of the Beast* and Fadia
Faqir's *Nisanit,* were both written *on* the course.) It's delicious to handle
Kurt's book, in its turquoise-and-cinnamon dust-jacket, with his own photos
of a deep-Texas township on the front and a photo of him on the back,
glinting saturnine and watchful. For the present MA group it's the best
evidence of what can be done. '*A Book*', I proclaim, and Graham echoes the
phrase half-ironically, as though testing the value of this possibly ephemeral
fruit.

Three pieces to be workshopped, two by Marian, one by Tracy. No longer
unnerved by her doldrum of the late winter/early spring, Marian is writing
lots and with a new edge to her always soberly lifelike fictions of the present
time. She hankers to write for theatre and has done a short piece about

three men in 'a mental hospital, but this need not be explicit'. They're all dependent, uncertain. One knows it all, including the Freudian meaning of leaving a room or wedging the door open. At the end he's falling apart, smoking furiously, panickily analysing himself: '[MOVES FROM CHAIR ONTO THE FLOOR] I move to a lower level . . . I seem to be sinking . . .', while the other two cuddle like child and mother. This is ambiguous, wryly comic, unlike anything she's shown before. In discussion Philip draws on his experience as actor and stage-writer and emphasizes that the 'mental hospital' is more symbolic than documentary: 'What have we got here? Three actors in a space'– that is, the play can open in almost any direction as a parable of people struggling to be sure of themselves. (He thinks it should be longer.)

Her story is virtually interior monologue: a woman talks to herself while having her hair done by Sandra at Short 'n' Curlies. She's fed up, aching for a change, any change, in her stale relationship – longing to be comforted ('I'd like a bed in here') – dourly ironic as a cover for hurt. To her man friend as he departs on a business trip: 'I promise not to kill the plants, don't worry about it.' Graham remarks on the humour in both pieces, and suggests that we're all writing more of that now, compared with the autumn. Certainly this was true at Clapdale, where writing very much *to* each other made us entertain more. (Think how much comedy is collaborative: The Pythons, Hall and Waterhouse, Galton and Simpson, Clement and La Fresnais – but not the best comic writer now, Victoria Wood.)

Tracy's story is a revision of an earlier one. No title (of course). A woman extremely close to her bracingly sceptical sister goes to live with her boy-friend. One night she's raped (described with ghastly force and not a trace of sadomasochism). Distraught, she turns not to Danny but to Mica. In version one this crucial move had been told in a way that loaded the story against the man, and I cited Lawrence's idea in 'Morality and the Novel': 'The novel is the highest example of subtle inter-relatedness that man has discovered . . . When the novelist puts his thumb in the scale, to pull down the balance to his own predilection, that is immorality.' Now Tracy's story has become subtle – 'impartial'; the narrator just has this long-rooted cama-raderie with her sister and that is what counts in her crisis. In this version Danny is still a lightweight – 'goofy', lovable, 'a wild dreamer'. But he does not *fail* his girlfriend. It's a classic case of how perfect one's touch must be. When a story has reached its best state, the events and personae speak for themselves and we are not suaded agin or for them.

12 June

A sample of work arrives from a Nigerian who's already applied, for 1992–3. A short novel called starkly *Slums*, published in the Heinemann African Library. It seems fully achieved – staccato, precise, full of well-imitated speech, in an un-English that smacks strongly and consistently of its own culture. On the dust-jacket the author is fleshy-faced, sturdy, deep black. So, with luck, in two years' time the course will have its first member from that huge, motley continent.

13 June

A poem for a change, by David, who (like Anne from Scotland and Graham) is part-time, i.e. one workshop per week for two years instead of two per week for one. David's work as a teacher – adviser in Cheshire uses his time very fully and he's remained slightly to one side of the group – no Clapdale, no video-viewing sessions, fewer coffees. He's imperturbable about this, steadily producing his remarkably idiomatic and actual rhyming poems. Today's, 'Rhoda Hood Tells A Bedtime Story', unfolds playfully: a granny dresses up in old-fashioned mittens, mob cap etc., to enact the Red Riding Hood story with her granddaughter.

> You'd look close: 'Grannie, what big teeth you have',
> As with my tongue I slide my dentures out . . .

For 'slide' David wanted to use 'pluff' but couldn't find it in any dictionary. I confirm it from 40-year-old memories of using it for blow-piping rice grains from glass tubes at classmates. The last two verses stunningly symbolize the wolf as mortal illness creeping up on the old woman:

> The wolf has settled on me like a fog.
> I smother, Rachel, in his matted fur.
> His scent is leaf mould,
> Thick moss, water squeezed from a rotten log.

> My ending's where he'll rise to devour me,
> Be a blaze of teeth and a blur of claws.
> Pass it on, Rachel,
> Tell it your daughter. Make it her story.

I raise the question of what the *gest* is in those last two lines – that invaluable idea of Brecht's which I should have found reason to bring into the workshops long ago: the fusion of 'gist' and 'gesture', the meaning of a passage as epitomized in the behaviour which would accompany the speaking of it, the mind-set embodied in the tone. *How would Granny say that*? With mordant irony, as though to say 'Go on, Rachel – just you terrify *your* daughter, just you *do* that – it's best she knows – isn't it?'?

A story by Jon, 'Play Ball', about masturbation, a mother's discovery that her son has become sexual, his best friend letting him down (causing him to break a leg). The streams in the narrative come and go with insouciant ease, as though a pianist were composing variations as the fancy took him, trusting his intuitions. As a result, I suggest – or possibly as a result – one of the two deepest matters, the mother's upset, goes for too little, is badly narrated. Jon, with his usual lack of defensive ego, makes a note to develop that crux. A fine point in the narrator's fall out of a tree: just before, he hears 'a quick rustling', sees nothing, then falls. This is never explained, the story ends 'I didn't know.' It works, not as a wilful mystery but as a symbol for the tremor of danger/betrayal/uncertainty at this turning in his life.

Months and months ago the group, led by Philip, conceived of an anthology of their stories/poems, to be well produced and sold in bookshops. Not to pour cold water on the poor dears, I went along with this, my mind sinking at memories of racking efforts to launch magazines and booklets, days and days turning the handles of duplicators, hundreds of letters and phone calls to drum up money, thousands of hours reading swathes of contributions – most of it for results on so small a scale. Now fruition may be approaching. Of various agents/publishers/funding bodies approached with a dummy volume set, printed, and hand-stitched by Philip, one has replied practically: John Killick of Littlewood Arc, one of the top five small presses (who are to publish my next book). On 22 May he visited us, gave us a thorough seminar on publishing and accepted the plan for the book, suggesting further that each student should also contribute a piece on how the course has gone for them/what it's meant to them, to widen the public for the book and make it distinctive. These pieces have mostly been written. The finance works out at £1,500 to produce the book: £500 from the university, £400 from North-West Arts, the balance from the Hamlyn Trust (John to approach them). Today, as we're about to break for coffee, the University Planning Officer phones to say that (a) we may well get two permanent half-time lecturers for next year, (b) we may well get funding for the book (which will count as a research project by the CW Unit). Good news is so rare – good money-news smacks of manna on the long trek to Canaan. We go over in high feather to the Greasepit – the Cartmel College 'bistro' where we usually have coffee. It's one of the few places known to me which has a system, most active in the winter, for *generating cold*. Today there's a notice at the hot servery: 'Please Stir Beans to Prevent Crust Forming'. We sit at our circular table, overlooking what was planned in 1968 as a beer garden, humming and buzzing with the good news – or benign mirage? – then go back to discuss the latest batch of draft pieces for The Book.

Anne from Scotland's is *about* the task of writing the piece itself – treated as a typical writer's job: 1,000 words for an imminent deadline: 'I type up on the screen "For me, the Lancaster experience continues", then sit back staring at it and conclude that it is a singularly unmeaningful sentence. The winking green eye of the cursor mocks my effort and the message at the top of the screen "Page 1, Line 1 of 52" starkly informs me of the long, bleak, bare road ahead.' Words here that would have been gibberish to most writers even five years ago. The others absolutely recognize such sensations. All the piece will need is a little trimming (fewer adjectives).

Jon's piece characteristically teems with information (the group now treat him as their scholarly memory) and works by commenting on all that sage advice to writers, from Faulkner, Pound, Joyce Carol Oates, John Updike . . . Marian's is a selection from her diary since 11 April 1990: 'Leicester. Got accepted on the MA course! UNBELIEVABLE. Unfit for anything but mowing the lawn. Took bubbly to Simon and Helen's and celebrated with a meal in Que Pasa.' None of us had expected a piece in diary form. It nicely mixes the professional and the private: 'Monday 11 February 1991. Work gone for a Burton. Spend days inert, just thinking. In love again, yes. When will I be able to write? What doesn't help is that HE has written a story!' Jon comments that this is of the essence – he, like the others, came here thinking, All I'll do this year is *write*. How wrong that was! Which is obvious, and absolutely understandable. What Marian's diary also gives me (after a month or two's uncertainty) is the form for this piece of mine, whose demands are now clawing at me in the small hours (5,000 words, by 1 July).

17 June

I walk downstairs and through this building (Lonsdale Hall, a separate block at the north end of the campus) to a xerox machine Anne's discovered in Visual Arts on the ground floor – no more trudging through drizzle or wind to the Law Department. The way through the Sculpture Studio is marked by a double line of yellow tape on the floor, zig-zagging between plinths with humpy white plaster figures, turntables with heads, inscrutable draped shapes, a suspended polyp of polythene on which someone has just dribbled runny ultra-marine paint. It's nice to mix with all this fruity clutter – and familial, since CW is now in the School of Creative Arts with Visual Arts, Theatre Studies and Music – and immediately practical, since we now want a designer for the Book and will seek one through Visual Arts. On my way back with a swathe of photostats, the paint has filmed over evenly, creating a blue sac, a mid-air jellyfish.

18 June

A chunk of Graham's novel – 'chunk' because he splits off the latest dozen pages, often in mid-sentence. This week's starts on p. 113 – 'into him. "And I'm going to leave the fucking bank," he shouted.' After nine months we know what he means, especially today when his gist is a scene between a couple who've only just met and are as intent on setting up a public meeting against racism as on their love-making. A fortnight ago the balance was almost absurdly in favour of the politics. Marian (who's become Graham's female conscience) led the criticism of this. The scene's transformed: the couple's fond intimacy is now quite richly suggested. Graham is a master adaptor and improver. Two years ago, when he started the course (and was then interrupted by my year off on study leave), his material was an awkward thriller, being written alternately with another of the same. Now it's a true novel, with audacious jump-cuts between the characters' lives and expert cartoon scenes of desperate modern history. The sequence now a byword among us is the one set in *a urological clinic in Tashkent.*

Tracy's piece for The Book, 'The Hardest Work', lucidly analyses how the group's criticizings slowly evolve into an enhanced version of *one's own self-critical faculty.* All I demur at is one or two plaudits for the group (and me) which would strike the reader as flank-rubbing.

Marian has put in a group of poems – rare for her. Precise, stripped-down, semi-lyrical notes on the irk of being emotionally dependent on your loved one(s). 'And me' raises, like many pieces this year, an issue of gender. We assume the narrator's female because the poet is. Then how do we read the middle verse?

> You wanted to be taken out
> Like a pet
> Fondled, fed, carried to bed
> Kissed and worshipped at
> Which he does

This 'you' is presumably a woman, who's replaced the narrator as her ex's girlfriend. Then how do we read verse 1? 'I snore too much, didn't cook for you' and so on. Does this mean that the two women in the triangle are bisexual and the other woman used to be in a lesbian relationship with the narrator? I suggest it doesn't matter, that the essence of the poem is painful problems between three people of whatever gender. Marian says no, she wanted the pampered 'you' to be definitely a man, since that's what men expect. We don't have an ideological set-to about this.

20 June

Philip's been struggling for months to cramp his novel together, as the limbs of a chair or table must finally be clinched into a set that stands up and will last. He's been struggling even to write the bloody words. Now he's put in some crackling sequences. Bill Shakeskyne, a pirate TV journalist, is covering the big match between L'Bird Port and Bad Croak, 'selecting shots from a dozen or so networks dotted round the ground. These he merged into a 3D signal, then bolted on a commentary in Servo-Croak, filched from a neighbouring hack.' The pieces so wittily and energetically deploy Philip's fascination with up-to-date (even beyond-date) media techniques that I concentrate on urging him to write-write-write in veins like that, shoot cansful of material (keeping half an eye on the overarching narratives) – then, after a brainstorming month or so, take it all into the cutting-room and edit.

An oldish story of Marian's that I first saw as evidence supporting her application. A fine scenario about how class and schooling start to split 10-year-old girls' friendship. Quite a few clichés – she no longer uses those; quite a few authorial prompts – ditto.

June accelerates, becomes uncontrollable, 'soft sift in an hour- glass'. The design man in Visual Arts, an old friend who did the first Lancaster Literature Festival programme 15 years ago, has found us a final-year student to design the cover for The Book. She asks us to prime her by means of a core image from each of our pieces, which produces a mad list of things like 'She floats out of the train on a balloon' and '27 years in bed'. She settles for butterflies, and asks for a strip of passport mug-shots for each of us to collage into parts of the design.

In the remaining Tuesday and Thursday we workshop three of Philip's sonnets, meaty poems in which he always uses just *one* rhyme-sound; for example in 'To . . .': sweet/sweat/what/blot/let/eat/meat/met/guillemot/knot/net/neat/swot/sweet. A poem of David's, for his daughter Megan, rich in home detail: on ironing, 'Underwear grows in mounds around/Me on the green carpet' – a split phrase there, between one line and the next, of the kind I've been gently badgering him to do away with throughout the year; he politely goes on treating this as my blind spot. Two pieces of Marian's (a monologue, the start of a story) about prostitutes. When someone asks her about her sources, she replies unforgettably, 'Well, a friend of mine's a prostitute . . .'

On June 27, after two and a half full hours in which the course reaches no climax but just runs out of time, we drive a mile west to meet Anne at Thurnham Mill for farewell food and drink, pots of mussels in a wine sauce, salads, Ruddles, lager, Campari. The gritstone building, put up at the end of the French Wars as the canal from Preston reached out towards Glasson, Lancaster, Kendal, was converted in the spring. Black wings of thunder-rain spread over the north of Morecambe Bay and lower Lunesdale. South into the Fylde it's serene, Mediterranean. Around 2 pm people are slipping away, to pack, to type some more, to resume their paid work. A swan sails eastward out of sight between beds of rushes and yellow iris. We'll keep in touch – student writers from 20 years ago are now among our permanent friends. But as a group working together week in week out, engaging minds as nearly as can be, weighing each other's words as scrupulously as discovered eggs before returning them to the nest, this is it – this is the finish.

Notes

1 Jon was one of the seven postgraduate writers working with me for the degree of MA at Lancaster University in 1990–1. Each year the course members meet twice a week from October to June (or once a week for two years if they are part-time)

for the best part of a morning or afternoon, to discuss previously-circulated photo-stats of the students' work-in-progress. That is what the course consists of – no lectures, no seminars, no exams or tests. (In September the folder of completed work by each student – in effect, a book – is marked by the external and internal examiners, that is, given a distinction, pass, resubmission or fail. Nobody has ever failed.) From time to time a professional writer comes to take the workshop, having been sent well in advance a set of pieces by all the students; Kazuo Ishiguro has visited us, and Maggie Gee, Iain Crichton Smith, Alastair MacLeod, Bernard MacLaverty, Carol Ann Duffy, Graham Mort, Russell Hoban, Graham Swift, James Simmons and Hugo Williams.

2 A guideline is a stimulus to a piece of writing there and then, suggested by the tutor, who also does the writing. (When I set one, I do my best not to have thought of it more than a few minutes before the session.) After a stint of any-thing from a few minutes to an hour we read aloud our pieces and discuss them. The idea is to vary the experience of the course; to give some practice in carrying out what is virtually a commission; and to use our time if not enough work has been handed in for an ordinary workshop. Originally I had a rather anarchistic or libertarian horror of using such deliberate stimuli. Then I went to a workshop taken by the playwright Stephen Jeffreys for two winters at the Brewery Arts Centre, Kendal, and found his guidelines (which he used most weeks) wonder-fully creative. It turned out that work done to order and against time was as likely to go well and to be characteristic of yourself as work done at your own sweet will.

3 A guideline in stages gives writers practice at planning larger pieces, managing time-jumps, shaping their work in sequences or chapters, and so on. A very short first stage (a few images or phrases jotted down in a minute or two) can be used to warm up. You can give out the whole guideline at the start, so that the earlier parts are written under the arch of the whole conception, including its end; or you can give out one stage at a time, as practice in managing an unforeseen change of direction which asserts itself in mid-work. On this occasion I gave out the whole guideline at the start.

Index